As I Saw It
A Collection of Short Stories on Rochester and the Taft Family

By
Justin Taft

To John and Edie
Hope you enjoy the
stories of my life.

Justin Taft

ISBN: 1-4140-5384-3 (e-book)
ISBN: 1-4140-5382-7 (Paperback)
ISBN: 1-4140-5383-5 (Dust Jacket)

Library of Congress Control Number: 2003099706

This book is printed on acid free paper.

Printed in the United States of America
Bloomington, IN

1stBooks - rev. 02/04/04

The author's ancestors at the home of my Grandfather William W. Taft enjoying a Sunday afternoon with friends, 1920.

Mr. and Mrs. Justin Taft on their wedding day.
December 20, 1947

Introduction: By Mrs. Justin Taft

In the Beginning: For Better and Not Worse

In the spring of 1947, I was a student nurse at Memorial Hospital in Springfield, Illinois. On March 12th, my friend Martha asked me to double date with her the following weekend. Martha's date was Lyle. She had met Lyle while working on a medical floor when he was admitted with a severe sore throat. Lyle had been visiting with *all* the student nurses and promised each of them a dinner date after he was discharged from the hospital. His date with Martha was set and he suggested that she ask a girlfriend to go along with them, since his best friend was available for a 'double date'. "No, I do not go on blind dates!" was my flat reply to Martha's invitation. I remained adamant for several days but she persisted until I finally relented and said, "Yes, I'll go".

Lyle relayed this message to his friend and their conversation ended like this: "Now, Lyle, you know Martha, but I've never seen her friend, so let's agree to do this – if I don't like my date, we'll go to a movie and straight home! If I approve of her I'll suggest that we go out to the Rochester Homecoming Dance!"

On March 19, the two boys arrived at the nurse's dormitory. From our upper front window, we could see Lyle and his friend, Justin Taft, striding up the walk. They were very nice and asked us what we would like to do. Our fertile minds could only think of going to a movie. My blind date, Justin, said, "We could go to a dance if you two young ladies would prefer. Our annual homecoming is being held tonight." To the dance, we went and enjoyed our evening very much! We dated through the summer and into the fall, when we found ourselves planning a spring wedding. I had a wedding gown laid away in November to start the preparations.

By the second week of December, Justin said that his folks were going to Arizona for the winter months and he was wondering if we could be married before they left! We finished the preparations in one week and were married on the 20th of December. Justin's mother and father left for Arizona on Monday December 22, 1947, and I went back to work!!! In December of 2003, we will have been married for 56 years and I cannot imagine life without him.

Family Life

When one lives in the midst of a large family, there is always someone to love. In our home, there were hugs to give and joys to share along with tears to dry, and disappointments to ease. When two more hands were needed there was also someone to help.

I was always busy cooking food to set in front of their faces or I was stuffing their minds with values of morality, character, truth and plain common sense. All the while, Justin was working hard to provide the wherewithal to cover necessities.

We all had a deep love for one another but when we disagreed, we each gave all we had to the fray. Yet, when it was over, I do not remember any one of us held a grudge. We were not perfect by any means but we stuck together. Here are a few tales from the memory bank of one whose cup continues to 'runneth over'. I was a wife and mother, a full-time employee as a registered nurse and a part of whatever Justin was into at the time. He farmed for the first fifteen years we were married. Then he became involved with politics and our world began turning a little faster

Creative Problem-Solving: Booking a Flight for the Tuxedo

Justin always wanted me to go with him to political events. I was happy to go whenever possible. Justin had held several township and county elected offices. At the time of this instance, he was running for Clerk of the Illinois Supreme Court. I was director of nursing at a local nursing home. I left work at mid-afternoon to hurry home and change clothes before driving with Justin up to Chicago for a 6:30

PM formal dinner at the Conrad Hilton Hotel. Justin never wore his tuxedo in the car so that it would not become wrinkled. We had driven about 70 miles north to the outskirts of Bloomington when he asked me if I was sure, I had put his tuxedo in the car trunk and I told him, "No, I know I didn't because I thought you did". We were close to the

Mardell Taft, RN on the job

halfway point of our drive to Chicago, so it was impossible to turn around and go back home to get his suit and have any hope of arriving at the dinner on time. We began problem solving aloud. I suggested we turn back to Bloomington and buy a new tuxedo. Justin said nothing, but suddenly he turned off at the next exit and stopped at the first gas station. He ran inside and I could see him frantically making telephone calls. He came back with a big grin and got into the car. He said, "It's all taken care of." He had called the desk of a commuter air service that flew into Meigs Field Airport on Lake Michigan, near downtown Chicago. He had asked if they would convey his tuxedo aboard the next flight, scheduled to depart in thirty minutes. They agreed to transport the suit. Justin then phoned our son George and asked him to drive the suit into the airport as soon as possible. When we drove into Chicago, we turned off Lakeshore Drive to Meigs Field and there was his tuxedo, on a hanger and ready for him to pick up. Best of all there was no charge for this unusual service! We could relax and enjoy our evening.

When political events were in Chicago, we would typically stay until 11:00 PM or 12:00 midnight. Then we would then drive 200 miles to our home in Rochester, arriving at 2:00 or 3:00 AM. Then we would wake up the next morning and get to work at the usual time. Some weeks we may have done that two or three times! We learned to prepare ahead of time as much as possible. I had made sure all my purses were equipped with the necessary articles from nail files to aspirin. One day the Governor of Illinois said that Justin Taft always beat him to the meetings, even though he drives his car and I fly in an airplane!

A Cowboy in the TV-Teepee: "They're Getting' Away!'

In the early 1950s, like many American families, we purchased our first television set. It was black and white with a thick convex glass front screen. One Saturday afternoon I was working in the kitchen while our eldest son George, 5-years-old, was watching a Cowboy Movie with his brother Jim, 3-years-old in the adjacent family room.

Since this room had the television in it, Justin took to calling it the 'TV Teepee'.

The author and family in 1963

As hard as it is to believe today, it was normal at that time for many parents to buy bee-bee guns for boys of that age! In keeping with that tradition of insanity, we had given George one such weapon for the preceding Christmas.

As I cooked and cleaned in the next room, little did I know that George was emulating the cowboys in western movies of that era by having his gun at his side. As the bad guys rode hard over a hill and the 'posse' lost sight of them, George got upset and in his excitement yelled, "Oh no! They're getting away!!" which was followed by a loud crack. I ran in to check on the boys only to find a smoking TV with a cracked glass screen! Seated on the couch, both boys were dumbfounded, looking as shocked as I was! When I asked what had happened, Jim said, "George shot the bad guys because they were getting away!"

The danger of the bee-bee gun had struck home to me! The gun was put away for a later time. I was only thankful that no one's eye had been shot out! And as for the TV, well as expensive as televisions were then, Justin said we'd just do without one for a while. Sometimes we wonder if that was not wisdom beyond our knowledge!

When the Kitchen Lights Blinked and Blinked

It was late afternoon and preparations for the evening meal were in process. As I worked, I began to notice the lights would blink quite often. It was something that had never happened before. Our two boys, George 5 years old and Jim 3 years old, were playing in the basement with the baby kitchen and several of their toys. I could follow their activities by their conversation floating up the steps into the kitchen. When the lights continued to blink and the boy's conversation ceased, I started down the steps to investigate. We had been painting and the evening before the brushes were left to soak in a pan of water so we could easily begin our task again at the proper time. Upon reaching the bottom of the steps, I saw both boys leaning over looking into the clothes dryer in serious conversation.

Jim: "Is she dry yet?"

George: "No, I'll have to run it again." With this, George shut the door and turned on the dryer. Lo and behold, the lights blinked! "What do you have in there?" I asked.

George: "The kitten's wet and we're just drying her out, Mom."

Thank goodness, they could not wait more than a couple of rotations before their curiosity made them check to see if she was dry! The poor little kitten was hanging on for dear life with her claws firmly inserted in the holes of the dryer drum. After rescuing her from her plight the boys were asked why they had done this to our little kitten and they quickly explained, "We painted her with the paint brush and when we saw how wet she was we were afraid you would be mad. We knew you dried everything in the dryer so we put her in, but she didn't like it and on top of it all she was still wet." I gathered the boys and we worked together to clean the paint off the kitten and dried her with a towel – petted her and loved her until she was not afraid any more. Then we all went upstairs where closer supervision would prevent any more mishaps.

This episode was repeated around our town and the boys had quite a time living it down. I felt it certainly was great that it turned out as it did. Even the kitty was unhurt. It proved to me that I could not leave them alone very long without checking on their activities, especially if the lights started blinking.

"I Believe I'll Go Again, Dad."

After the birth of our second child, James, we proudly sent out birth announcements to all our friends and relatives. These 'baby cards' depicted a baby boy piloting a cute little blue airplane through the clouds. On the inside were recorded all of little Jim's vital statistics. A few extra cards remained and I had tucked them away inside his 'baby box', which held his birth mementos.

When Jim was three years old, the family attended the Fourth of July celebration in Rochester. After a round of ice cream cones, we came to the rides. Jim was 3 years old and was eager to take his first ride on the little train by himself, but when we came to the gate, he got a little scared. Although Jim was very unsure about all of this, he finally accepted our encouragement and sat upright in his train seat, looking stoically straight ahead. We, on the other hand, stood by watching closely to see if he was frightened, enjoying himself, or just bored. His expression never changed. At length, the train stopped and we hurried toward him to see what he thought of his train ride. When he saw us coming, without cracking a smile, he said, "I believe I'll go again, Dad!" We were both so relieved, Justin ran for another ticket and we watched him do an exact repetition of the first ride.

Years later, when Jim was eighteen, he joined the Air National Guard and flew F-4 Phantoms. After retiring from military service, he became a Commercial Airline Pilot. We used to wonder if it all started on that first solo train ride at the Fourth of July celebration! However, I was recently cleaning the attic of our house and came upon the children's 'baby boxes'. As I looked through the precious contents, one of Jim's birth announcement cards appeared. The site of baby Jim in an airplane from the onset was startling! The whole family got a good chuckle about his 'pilot cards'.

Do I Get the Job? - The Teacher is Interviewed by a Six-Year-Old

Justin was president of the Rochester School Board in 1958 when Nancy was 6-years-old and ready to start first-grade. One August day, Justin went up to the school to check on something the board was trying to complete before the school year started in two weeks. Nancy went with him and played on the swings and playground equipment while her Dad was busy. She noticed a light on in an open basement window and went over to peer into the classroom. A teacher greeted her and the conversation went something like this:

Teacher: "Hello little girl, what's your name?"

Nancy: "I'm Nancy Taft and I'm going to be in the first grade when school starts this year."

Teacher: "Isn't that great! I am a first grade teacher. This is my classroom and I am decorating it to be pretty and interesting. Maybe you'll be in my class!"

Nancy: "What kind of stuff do you teach?"

Teacher: "I teach children to start reading, writing the alphabet and counting. We will be reading some exciting stories about the adventures of Dick and Jane. I am also planning to have lots of art; like painting, drawing, and coloring. We will also practice dancing, singing songs and playing musical instruments like the triangle, drumsticks and tonette."

Nancy: "What's a tonette?"

Teacher: "It's kind of like a flute, a long instrument that you blow into while moving your fingers to cover different holes along the tube."

Nancy: I'd sure like to be in your class because you seem really fun and nice, but I can't be your pupil, since my Dad already put me in that old teacher's class."

Teacher: "Well maybe if you tell him that we met and enjoyed talking with each other you can switch over to my classroom."

Nancy: "It won't work. You do not know my Dad. You see, he is the president of the school board and he says it is my first year so it is important that I have a really good teacher. Since you're a brand new teacher he doesn't want me in your classroom."

Later that evening we were sitting at the kitchen table having our evening meal when Nancy announced: "I met the prettiest teacher up at the school today and she asked me my name. I told her who I was and that I would be in first-grade this year. She said that maybe I would be in her class because she will be teaching first-grade. After I talked to her, I decided that she was a lot of fun, so I told her that I would rather be in her class but Dad had already put me in the other teacher's room. I explained that he wanted the best teacher for my first year of school and he didn't know yet if the new girl knew how to teach."

Needless to say, after her father calmed down, the whole thing was discussed at a later time and it was finally determined that Miss Nancy would be in the young beautiful and fun teacher's class for first-grade. Justin also informed her that she must study hard, learn her lessons, behave as a young lady and make good grades on her report card or she would be in trouble! Nancy did study hard, made good grades and, yes, the new girl did teach well!

Nature Comes Indoors: Some Enchanted Bedroom

Starting in high school, Nancy developed a great talent for choosing tasteful items when we were re-decorating and would do painting, paper hanging, and the whole category of needs when improving a room. However, I drew the line on one job! In the summer of 1971, while home between her freshman and sophomore year of college, she announced that she wanted to redecorate her bedroom. She effusively described her plan for this project. First, she wanted to get grass-green shag carpeting then she would paint the walls *and* ceiling light blue. She would finish it off by hand painting the baseboard and part of the lower wall to represent grass, flowers and shrubbery. Higher aspects of the wall would have trees painted, replete with birds and butterflies. The crowning glory was the ceiling, which was to have a sun and clouds!!! She even wanted to make some of the trees and bushes 3-D by outward projections constructed of paper mâché on wire!

Wouldn't you know that while looking at a 2003 magazine the other day, there was Nancy's room complete with a ceiling painted sky-blue with clouds!! I just did not recognize a good idea when I heard it thirty years ago!

Act III: Theatrical Drama as Nancy and J.T. Go on Stage

Nancy had an unstoppable imagination. She was eleven and J.T. was five when she announced the presentation of a play that evening. The rest of the family was to gather in the living room for the two thespians presentation at 7:00 PM. They rehearsed all afternoon. The play began as they embarked upon a journey. As their trip began, they experienced amazing adventures during the first and second 'Acts' which concluded as they boarded a train. For "Act III', Nancy had placed four dining room chairs in a row to represent a train. At days end they settled into sleeping berths and went to sleep. When morning came, they proceeded to the dining car for breakfast. Nancy had plastic food from her toy chest out to represent the meal they would eat. However, when she handed J.T. his breakfast plate he had exited the stage! Exasperated, Nancy announced an intermission and went to find J.T. We waited… and waited…, and waited, but no one came back. Finally, we all left the living room to see what had happened and found them in the kitchen. Nancy was lecturing J.T. about unprofessional behavior, while he sat calmly eating a bowl of Fruit Loops with milk! When asked what was going on, J.T. said, "It was time for breakfast, so I decided I was hungry. Anyway, I'm just doing what she had told me to do in that old play!"

Terror on Wheels: The Go-Cart Toddler

The children were all home during the summer and we had just finished eating lunch. The three boys had gone outside and the two girls stayed in the house. As I stood at the kitchen sink washing the dishes, I could partially see the boys in the barnyard. George, fourteen, and Jim, twelve, had just gotten a go-cart. I was anxious, although Justin had spent considerable time going over safety precautions with them. All of a sudden, I looked out the window and beheld J.T., who was only three, driving the go-cart all by himself! Worst of all, he was headed down our driveway, which connected to a four-lane highway. There was little time to do anything, but I ran out into the lawn after him all the same. As I ran across the lawn, he reached the end of the driveway and I screamed! Lo and behold – J.T. commanded the steering wheel like a pro and performed a U-Turn back into our barnyard!! I did not know whether to hug him or scold him, but instinctively held him close to me. All three boys were in trouble for that stunt. Only later, could we look back on the event and marvel, even laugh, at the image of our three-year-old stunt driver!

Daddy's Girl: Biddies Cleans-Up

One morning as I came down the staircase, I heard the rattle of paper and the thump of a box hitting the kitchen floor. Entering the kitchen I encountered Carolyn, then 3-years-old (and our youngest), who was trying to navigate the broom. She was cleaning up Rice Krispies cereal that had spilled to the floor all around her! The broom was three times taller than Carolyn was so her efforts were awkward, at best. She was muttering under her breath, "I have to get this mess cleaned up before Daddy gets home!" Well, her Daddy was due any minute. So Nancy, 12-years-old, took the broom from her and swept up the intended snack. As Nancy was discarding the mess she said, "Yes, we have to clean it up or Daddy won't take you to the New Berlin Fair (Sangamon County Fair) tonight." This evening's outing to the county fair had been anticipated all week! Carolyn drew herself up with all her dignity and replied: "My father will, too, take his little daughter to the fair! I'm his Little Biddies!" This was Justin's pet name for Carolyn that we all heard each time he came through the door asking, "Where's my 'little biddies'?" and Carolyn would run to meet him for a big hug.

Yes, Carolyn did get to go the county fair and she rode the Ferris Wheel with her Daddy after which time he bought her a real snack – an ice cream bar, coated in chocolate and covered with nuts! This closeness has continued through the years and is still present today between Carolyn and her 'Daddy'. All parents have special ties to each child and so did Justin, but this was a particular tie between him and his youngest daughter, Carolyn.

Preface

I have had a very interesting life and feel strongly that the Lord has had a hand in my long life, good memory and other good fortunes. Stories have always been part of my life and I enjoy sharing a good tale. During story-telling sessions, people have asked why I have not written a book. I have tried to recall many early memories and stories and hope others find some redeeming qualities in this effort.

I was born in 1924. Calvin Coolidge was in the White House. Prohibition reigned in America but could not constrain the energy and vitality of the Roaring Twenties. Much of Illinois and the United States were economically and culturally agrarian. America was recovering from World War I, known then as "The Great War."

Air flight was in its infancy and automobiles were still foreign, frightful machines for much of the country. People traveled long distances by railroad, and horses pulled America's plows. As a child, I never knew of air conditioning or television. Personal computers and the Internet were decades away. At a time when people shared party-line phones and used operators to make connections, cell phones and worldwide communications were beyond comprehension.

The names of Charles Lindbergh, Adolph Hitler and Dwight Eisenhower were little known to the world. Blitzkrieg, storm troopers, gas chambers and holocaust were unknown terms. Few people had heard of Pearl Harbor, the Coral Sea or Hiroshima. Fascism was on the rise in Europe; Communism was in its infancy; and Isolationism dominated American thinking.

I lived through three great events of the 20th Century: The Great Depression, World War II and the transformation of the United States from an isolationist nation to the world's lone, dominant power. When I look back over my life, I feel blessed to have lived through this period of time. I feel like I have seen everything.

Throughout my life, I have tried in most situations to see the good, rather than the bad. Like everyone in my generation, I experienced the depths of an economic depression and realities of the world at war. These were surely difficult periods, but at the time people did not feel their lives were so terrible. People went on with their lives and raised families. I remember the hardships, but I also recall the fun we had and enjoy telling about the good times and the humorous moments.

As a person looks back and reflects on the events of life, one thinks of the many friends and acquaintances that played a part in making certain things happen. If time and space were not limited, I would attempt to recognize the many good people who made a great difference in my life. This is not possible, but I want to say thanks to all my wonderful friends for the inspiration and good times. Many friends have passed on, and I trust that those who remain know how much I appreciate their friendship. Thanks again.

This book is written so future generations will know more of the history of Rochester and one of its citizens who truly enjoyed living in and talking about this community. The biggest motivation for this book came from my family. They have heard the stories, but they asked me to write the stories for future reference. I thank my family for helping me be what I am. I hope this book serves as an inspiration to all that read it. Enjoy life, try to help others and love your fellow man.

January 29, 2004   Justin Taft

Acknowledgements

This book is dedicated to my family and many friends. Family has been important throughout my life, and I greatly appreciate the support my family has given me for eight decades. Family members urged me to write this book and without their encouragement, I might not have embarked on this project.

I want to acknowledge the one person in my life who probably knows my stories nearly as well as I do. For 56 years, my wife, Mardell, has shared her life with me, and I consider myself to have been very fortunate. She has either lived through many of the experiences in this book or heard the stories so often that she thinks she lived through them. Mardell and I have five children, as well as wonderful grandchildren and great grandchildren.

I am particularly thankful to the people of Rochester, Illinois where I have resided my entire life. Many of the stories in this book are about Rochester, particularly during its earlier days. I cherish the memories growing up on a farm and being a part of such a wonderful place as Rochester.

The actual writing of this book could not have been accomplished without the tireless assistance of my friend Bill McClain. Bill spent countless hours listening to my accounts of life. He then helped me organize and transfer my oral stories to the written word.

William (Bill) McClain attended public schools in Waverly, Illinois. He received a botany degree from Eastern Illinois University and a masters in botany from Miami (of Ohio) University. Bill taught biology and science at Carlinville, Illinois and worked for a consulting firm. He later served as a field biologist and natural areas program manager for the Illinois Department of Natural Resources. Bill McClain writes for nature magazines and scientific journals.

Table of Contents

Life in Vermont and Massachusetts

No Way to Make a Living

In pre-revolutionary America, the Taft Family lived in Vermont for many years. They made their living by farming and taking people for rides on their sailing boat on Lake Champlain. They were also very interested in politics, and Josiah Taft served two terms in the Vermont legislature.

In 1828, my great grandfather, William made the long trip to Illinois where he built a home on the Illinois prairie. His parents, Josiah and Phoebe, remained in the small town of Ferrisburg, Vermont, with the rest of their children. The distance between family members was great and the likelihood existed that they might never see each other again. Their correspondence underscores their understanding of this concern.

They corresponded by letter, but some family members were not very diligent at answering letters they had received. Letters were very special and each day brought hope that a letter would arrive at the local post office. Family members in Ferrisburg were disappointed most days. A letter dated February 13, 1832 describes how someone went to the post office two or three times a week during the fall and winter months, but no letter arrived. The letters that were written almost beg other family members to come back home.

The few letters that arrived in Rochester spoke of bouts of loneliness and depression. It was easy to understand the loneliness. It was the midst of winter and Isaac, my great grandfather's youngest brother, had recently died. William's mother, Phoebe, is described as being "so lonely since Isaac's death that she can hardly compose herself." Another letter states: "You can't think how lonesome we all are." Other

1

families had left Ferrisburg for Illinois or Ohio, and the sentiment was growing to join the family in Rochester, Illinois.

Writing letters was not nearly as simple as it is today. A quill or feather was often used, and it had to be dipped in an ink well after every few words. Sometimes the ink would come off of the quill too quickly, creating a big black spot. Writing paper was also very hard to find. The lack of quality writing paper often caused some individuals to write on every little bit of space available, and then turn it and write at a right angle across the letter. This was difficult to read, but it was one way of getting the most out of the available paper.

In Vermont, life was difficult. The year 1816 would be remembered as "The Year Without a Summer". Frosts and hard freezes continued to occur throughout the summer and very few crops were raised. This unusually cold weather was due to volcanic dust present in the atmosphere due to the eruption of a volcano.

Life was particularly difficult for a family that made a living by farming in Vermont. A letter from 1834 states that they have raised just "a nuf to live on for the last two years." On May 15 of that year, a spring snowstorm left three to four feet of snow on the level ground. Some family members with sailing boats on Lake Champlain relied upon the income raised from renting their boats as pleasure crafts for tourists. The cold weather had greatly reduced that income, and their correspondence suggests they were considering selling their boats on Lake Champlain.

The weather, Isaacs's death, a smallpox epidemic and the departure of family and friends were taking their toll on the Vermont Taft's. When Isaac died in 1834 at the age of 10, he was buried in the Ferrisburg Cemetery. Moving to Illinois was discussed, but "father says we can't move until we do something with the land." Even Josiah, my great, great, grandfather, was thinking that it was time to leave Vermont.

Five years passed before the remainder of the Vermont Taft's moved to Rochester. Josiah Taft never left Vermont. He passed away in 1838 and was buried in the Ferrisburg Cemetery. His wife Phoebe made the long trip to Rochester in 1839 with two daughters and a son-in-law. Phoebe adjusted to her new environment on the prairie and lived for many years in Rochester. Her main reason for coming to Rochester was to help raise her grandchildren. She passed away in 1861 and was buried in the "burying grounds" on the Taft Farm.

Two early pioneers: My father, the first Justin Taft, is on the right with his twin brother, Jason. The yoke seen in this picture was brought from Vermont and remains in my possession. (Circa 1900)

Taft's were not the only ones who made the move from Vermont to Rochester, Illinois. The New England cold weather and rocky soils caused others to follow. The families of Samuel D. Slater, Munson Carter, Carter Tracy, John Sattley, Samuel Stevens and Christopher Stafford moved to Rochester in those early years and made great contributions to Rochester and Sangamon County.

The Village Blacksmith

The Taft's came to America from England early in the history of this country. Robert and Sarah Taft settled with their family in Mendon, Massachusetts in the year 1680. They had five sons, and all of them were industrious individuals who farmed or worked other occupations in the surrounding area. I am a descendent of Benjamin, the youngest son of Robert and Sarah Taft. President William Howard Taft was descended from Benjamin's brother, Robert Taft. The Taft family has grown and scattered all over the nation in the last three centuries, but they have not forgotten their ties to Mendon.

Marker stone at the Robert and Sarah Taft's original home site.

Since 1874, the Taft's have been holding reunions at Mendon. They occur every five years, and I have had the opportunity to go to two of these events. A stone, marking the location of a blacksmith shop operated by Caleb Taft at nearby Uxbridge was dedicated at one of the reunions I attended. Perhaps people will wonder why this shop was so special. It was this blacksmith shop that inspired Henry Wadsworth Longfellow to write the poem, "The Village Blacksmith". Generations of Americans have enjoyed this famous poem.

The shop building has been gone since 1920, but it was not destroyed. Henry Ford purchased the blacksmith shop and moved it to Greenfield Village in Dearborn, Michigan. It remains there to this day, along with many other historic buildings Henry Ford bought, such as the Wright Brothers' Dayton bicycle shop. I understand Greenfield Village is very nice, but I have never had the privilege of visiting or seeing the Caleb Taft blacksmith shop.

Caleb Taft was known for his work in the Mendon area, and his wife was widely known for her strength. She could pick up a full barrel of rum and drink out of the bunghole with ease. There were very few men and virtually no other women who were capable of such a feat.

Although little is written about Caleb Taft or the work he did, we do know that four generations of Taft's worked in the blacksmith shop and it was in operation for 120 years. Caleb Taft put shoes on oxen, and this required a sling to lift the animal off of the ground. That might seem to be a rather extreme measure, but oxen are not capable of lifting their legs like horses, so they have to be lifted off of the ground so shoes can be fitted on them.

The blacksmith shop has been gone from its original site for over 80 years, but stories about its history remain. Each reunion brings out these stories, but the most enduring story about this blacksmith shop is the poem by Longfellow. Millions of people have read and enjoyed Longfellow's poem, but few have known the poem's subject was the little shop owned and operated by Caleb Taft.

Early Days in Rochester

William W. Taft home on the "Ocean to Ocean" highway, ½ mile west of Rochester, built in approx. 1875

Early Rochester Businesses

The first store to operate in Rochester was owned by a man named Sam West. His store was located on the north side of where State street is now located. According to the daybook from his store, Sam West did a good business in corn whiskey, which went under the name "corn juice." Corn whiskey sold for 25 cents a quart, or 56 1/2 cents a gallon. Records show that Mr. West purchased three barrels of corn whiskey on May 17, 1838 from a local resident.

Munson Carter and Carter Tracy built many of the brick buildings in Rochester. They used these buildings for their grocery stores from about 1840 to 1880. Munson Carter was the first mayor of Rochester.

The old dirt road that came through Rochester was a big help to local businesses. It was called the Ocean-to-Ocean Highway or the Lincoln

Highway. It was a major road that brought a lot of traffic through town in the early days. It was the only way to get to Springfield until 1927 when the new paved road was built.

Every community had a livery stable to house the horses, and Rochester had two. One stable was run by the Ott family and was located north of Rainy's garage, at the southeast corner of North Walnut and Mill Street. The other stable was run by the Highmore family and was located on John Street, where the old post office was later built. Livery stables were an essential part of life in Rochester, but went out of business when automobiles came into common use.

Bert Wolford operated a hardware store. He also owned a steam tractor and did custom threshing for area farmers. His brother Sam worked in the store as a tinsmith. Most of Sam's business was making pipes and pieces for furnaces.

Hoopie Smith was a tinsmith in town. He made the copper steamer my grandfather Taft used to make suet pudding. People said Hoopie was able to work only one day a week because he was drunk the other six. He never changed his clothes, and usually wore them until they became pretty stiff. He was a very good tinsmith when he did work.

The Twist Brothers operated a brickyard in town for several years. It was located on the south edge of town. The source of clay for the bricks was located near the kilns. It was an ideal situation, and their business furnished the bricks used in the construction of many buildings in town. Additionally, they made field tiles used to drain many acres of local farmland. The brickyard closed in the 1920's, but the kilns were still present in the 1930s.

The biggest business operated by the Twists was a system of grain elevators. They owned 35 elevators in the surrounding area and were responsible for storing and shipping considerable amounts of grain. Some of their early elevators still stand. The other elevators

8

have been replaced by more modern structures. The Twist's later developed a telephone network to communicate between the home office in Rochester and their elevators. This system developed into the Rochester Telephone Company and was later sold to Bell Telephone.

Carol Rainy operated a garage and worked on most types of cars. His garage was located across the street from the Methodist Church. Besides working on cars, he had an avid interest in sailing boats. He bought a bus in 1936 and used it to transport school children. He also used his bus to take the school athletic teams to away games.

There were several doctors in Rochester during the early years. They were Dr. Babcock, Dr. Cantrall, Dr. McNeal, Dr. Wright, and his son, Dr. Lyman Wright. I stepped on a nail once, and my mother took me to Dr. Lyman Wright. My mother had been putting bacon on the wound to draw out the poison. Dr. Wright asked why she didn't put sour milk and bread on it instead of bacon.

H. D. Parker ran a drug store in Rochester where he sold all kinds of tonics and salves. He had a soda fountain many people enjoyed. Parker came to Rochester from Mt. Auburn and operated his store for fifty years. His business came to an end during the great fire of 1930 when half of the businesses burned down in Rochester.

Charlie Jones was a retired farmer who moved to Rochester and became the town's undertaker. His funeral home was located on the south side of the highway, across from the old Methodist Church. Mr. Jones had a horse-drawn hearse he used for the last time when my grandfather was buried. Charlie Jones was the grandfather of Wilson Park, the current funeral director in Rochester.

Kenny Jones operated a service station in Rochester for many years. It was a popular place when I was a child. He sold candy and other treats. He also bought punchboards from the candy company. A person had to pay 5 cents to punch out one of the holes. If you were lucky

Left to right, Old Mill, Jones's Undertaker Parlor and Blacksmith shop.

enough to win at this game, you could win up to five dollars.

Milton Green operated another service station. Milt always had a checker game going in his store and claimed he was the checker champion. Anyone who wanted to buy some gas might have to wait a while until the game was over or until an important move had been made. That way of doing business would never work today.

There were a number of grocery stores in Rochester in the early years, including Fannie Delay, Alphonso Eggleston and Gideon Oliver. These grocery stores were always located in uptown Rochester. Fannie Delay's store was advertised as the "Quality store", and it featured general merchandise. Eggleston's advertisement stated that they were dealers in "Staple and Fancy Groceries". They also had all kinds of fruit, nuts and vegetables. They were always in the market for poultry, eggs, butter and lard. Alphonso, who was known by his friends as Lonnie, advertised that: "I make a specialty high Grade flour. Try a sack of UnoFlour."

Gideon Oliver's grocery was a Clover Farm store that traded in general merchandise. The store featured Clover Farm products such as spices, salves, teas, and other merchandise. S. G. Richardson also had a grocery store in Rochester. His store featured staple and fancy groceries, hardware, boots and shoes, washing machines and churns. He also offered to pay the highest market price for poultry, eggs, butter and lard. His advertisement said: "Phone me for prices."

Two grocery store buildings built by early Vermont settlers Munson Carter and Carter Tracy. Bricks came from local brick kiln.

Another grocery store in Rochester was operated by Alvey Nichols and was located on the east side of John Street. His store was in the Odd Fellows Lodge building. Mr. Nichols made home deliveries of groceries in a steel-wheeled wheelbarrow every day.

Floyd "Red" Crowl operated a gas and oil truck in Rochester. He was the "Standard Oil Man" for the area. He had a bulk plant located next to the railroad tracks in town. The railroad would deliver a tank of gasoline and barrels of grease and oil that Red would sell and deliver to area farmers.

Chris Matthews also ran a bulk gas and oil truck in Rochester. His family suffered a terrible tragedy when an old coal oil stove caught the dress of his daughter on fire. Chris's wife tried to save the little girl, but mother's clothing also caught on fire and both of them died from their burns.

Jess Fowler's wife ran a restaurant in uptown Rochester, next to Oliver's "Clover Farm" grocery store. She served good home-style food. Chili was one of their specialties. Jess was the Swift Chicken man for the Rochester area.

The Twist Family

The Twist family came to Rochester in the early 1830s and figured prominently in the development of the town. In addition to owning many acres of farmland around Rochester, members of the Twist family were known to be good business people. They started several businesses in Rochester and Sangamon County. They were related to the Sattley's, another early Rochester family.

The Twists owned and operated a hardware store and the brickyard. Later, they developed a telephone system in Rochester that was eventually sold to Bell Telephone. The Twist's telephone company had 950 miles of wire and 390 subscribers. They advertised that their phone service was "second to none." The telephone system was originally built to operate one of their biggest business ventures, a group of grain elevators along railroads throughout the county. This system allowed the Twist's to communicate between their elevators and the headquarters at Rochester. Their peak operation occurred about 1915 when they owned and operated 35 elevators. A few of their elevators still stand to this day, but none are operational.

Not all of the Twist's remained in Rochester during the towns early years. News of the California gold discovery in 1849 reached

The Twist building, destroyed by fire in 1930. Upstairs on left was the Twist Telephone switchboard, lower left was G A Wolford, hardware, lower right was H D Parker, drugstore. Upper right was an early Masonic Lodge.

Rochester, and John Twist decided he would go to the gold fields and seek his fortune. He traveled overland by horse from Illinois to California. When he decided to return to Illinois, he did not want to return the way he had come. He took a ship from California to the Isthmus of Panama, walked through the jungle to the east coast and took another ship back to the United States, eventually reaching Rochester.

Two of the Twist brothers began visiting the St. Francis River valley near Earl, Arkansas about 1915. They soon began to buy parcels of farmland used to grow cotton and other crops. They bought more land each time they went to Arkansas. The expanding farm holdings caused them to move to Arkansas and establish the town of Twist. Eventually, they developed a large plantation with 17,000 acres.

It took a lot of people to farm the Twist's Arkansas plantation. Over

1,000 tenant families lived on the Twist land, and the Twists operated a store, sawmill and other businesses for use by the tenants. They operated the store like a "company store" common in the Appalachian Mountain coal mining area during this same era. The tenants were allowed to run a tab or charge their groceries. Their bill would be paid off when the work began in the cotton fields.

The Twists needed a foreman to supervise the work on the plantation. They asked a man from Rochester, "Crow" Durbin to come down to Arkansas and be their foreman. He spent nearly 20 years in Arkansas directing work on farms before returning to Rochester where he spent his final years. He told many stories of life on the Twist plantation.

The plantation tenants were allowed to cut timber for firewood and building materials on land owned by the Twist's. When the land was completely cleared, it would be farmed. The tenants got free firewood and the Twist's got their land cleared.

Few people in Rochester recognize the prominent role the Twist Family played in the early development of Rochester because the Twist's have been gone for many years.

Although the Twists left Rochester nearly a century ago, some family members maintained ties to Rochester. When Clarence Twist died in 1940, he wanted to be buried in the Rochester Cemetery. Clarence had grown up in Rochester and married a girl from Springfield. He was buried, according to his wishes, in the Rochester Cemetery and a large granite monument was placed for a headstone. His wife called in 1954, however, and said she didn't want to be buried in Rochester. She wanted to be buried in Earl, Arkansas and she was going to have Clarence moved to the cemetery there. This was done, but the large granite headstone was left in the Rochester cemetery.

For many years, the American Legion had wanted to dedicate a monument for the veterans from Rochester, but did not have the financial resources to purchase one. I called Mrs. Twist in 1955 and asked her if the Legion could have the monument. She said yes, so I had a monument company remove the Twist name and inscribe the symbol of the American Legion in its place. The monument was then moved to a location near the flagpole at the cemetery entrance. There are few people who know the monument's connection to the Twist Family. In the lower part of the monument there is an inscription stating, "donated by the C.C. Twist family".

Early Days of Gasoline Sales

We think nothing of going to a gas station for gasoline these days. Practically every town, regardless of size, has a self-service station that makes it easy for people to fuel their cars quickly.

It wasn't always this way. There were two stations in Rochester during the 1920s, a Shell station and the Standard Oil bulk plant operated by Floyd Crowl. The Shell Station was located in the center of town. When the new highway was constructed, most of the traffic no longer passed by the Shell Station and it soon went out of business.

The Standard Oil Bulk plant was located next to the railroad. Big storage tanks held the gasoline and oil, and grease was kept in big barrels inside of a storage shed. The railroad would deliver the gasoline to the bulk plant in tanker cars, and it would be unloaded into the storage tanks. A small tanker truck was used to haul the gasoline to the farms.

The Standard Oil man, Floyd "Red" Crowl, delivered gasoline to our farm. Instead of taking out a hose and pumping the gas as one might suspect, he measured the gasoline in a five-gallon bucket he carried to the tank. He used a funnel to pour the gasoline into the tank, and repeated the process until it was full or he had filled our order.

Red's measuring bucket was no ordinary bucket because it had markings on the side to indicate the various amounts of gasoline. Carrying a five-gallon bucket filled with gasoline, though, could be a little tricky at times. Red walked into the clothesline once, causing him to fall and spill all of the gasoline when he went down.

Gasoline wasn't the only petroleum product we bought from Red Crawl. He also sold kerosene that was used for lamps and axle grease we used on the farm machinery. Many of the early tractors also burned kerosene. Gasoline would be used to start the engine, and a valve would be turned to switch the engine to kerosene.

Most of the old bulk plants were torn down years ago, and no tractors burn kerosene these days. Only the older tractors burn gasoline, so mostly diesel fuel is now delivered to farms. There are few individuals who remember the days when gasoline was delivered to farms in five-gallon buckets.

Early Basketball

Few people would ever guess that the first basketball games in the Rochester Schools were played outdoors on a cinder court in about 1924. We did not have uniforms, so the boys played in their bib overalls and work boots. We didn't have any basketball hoops either; so two hoops were made by the local blacksmith, Chris Ginther, and nailed to the backboards on the posts. Any spectators who might show up stood along the sides of the court.

Some of the first games in Chatham were played in the town hall. It was a narrow building, about 25 feet wide and 50 feet long and had a pot-bellied stove at one end. During one game, the ball hit the stovepipe and knocked it to the floor. Dust and smoke went everywhere, and the game had to be stopped until some men put the pipes back together. Several of the men had gloves they had been using to shuck corn in the back pockets of their bib overalls, and they put these on before reassembling the stovepipe. After cleaning the floor, the game continued without any more incidents with the stove.

I recall another interesting basketball game occurred in Chatham. One of the players was running and started to stumble near the end of the court. When he hit the door at the end of the building, it flew open and he landed outside in a snowdrift. He wasn't hurt, so he brushed off the snow, closed the door and the game resumed.

Early "Rocket" team with "Orange and Blue" uniforms (Circa 1944) My brother, Arnold Taft, is second from left in the front row. The coach sitting next to Arnold is Maurice Scott, who later served as President of the Taxpayers Federation of Illinois for many years.

The early indoor games in Rochester were played in the basement of the Methodist Church. The room was not very large and the ceiling was only about 14 feet high. When shots were taken, the ball often hit the ceiling. The town bought the old WCTU Opera house and remodeled it to use for basket games and other events.

At that time, the grade school had red and black suits, and the high school had gold and purple suits. When the high school was built in

1937, it contained a new gymnasium that became the location for all of the basketball games. During a student assembly in the fall of 1937, the decision was made to change the school colors to "Orange and Blue", and to adopt the "Rockets" as the name for the school's teams.

Many years have passed since the first basketball games in Rochester. Believe it or not, my dad, Justin Taft Sr., kept the hoops made by Chris Ginther, and they were nailed to one side of our barn. We played many games at our home using these hoops. When the barn was torn down, I took these hoops and donated one of them to the Rochester Schools. This hoop is in the trophy case at the high school to this day.

Growth of Rochester

Rochester Schools

The Illinois Constitution of 1818 provided that section 16 of every township could be sold and the money derived from the sale could be used for the construction of schools. The first school built in Rochester was a two-room log cabin located on the south side of Main Street. This building was in the 100 block across from where the Masonic Building now stands. This school was built some time in the 1830s, and served as the school through the early 1840s. It is not known who built this early school. It also served as a community center where meetings and church services were held. It is likely that the community pooled their resources to finance the school construction.

The Taft Family has been associated with the Rochester Schools for many years. The first family member to be involved was Nancy Taft, who went to school and was trained to be a teacher at Ferrisburg, Vermont. She came to Rochester in 1839 to join her brother and other family members. Her training as a teacher proved valuable, for she became the teacher in the two-room log cabin schoolhouse during the winters of 1842 and 1843. School was only held during the winters during those early years.

The record is incomplete as to what happened to this early log cabin school. It may have served as a school for many more years, but it is also likely that another building was constructed for use as a school. The next building for which there is a record was built in 1885 at a cost of $4,000. This building served as the school until 1920, when it became the Masonic Temple.

Two Twist brothers, Clarence and Frank, went to this school and after

Rochester School House from 1885-1920

graduation, went to the University of Illinois. They were very good athletes, and soon were members of university athletic teams. Clarence was a member of the baseball team, and Frank was a member of the football team. Franks football team went undefeated for three straight

The 1920 Rochester School House

years. It was quite an honor to have two brothers from Rochester schools attending the University of Illinois.

A new school building was built in 1920, and I started classes there in the fall of 1929. There were six rooms in the school, including four upstairs and two in the basement. Also in the basement was the boiler room, where coal was used as fuel for heating. Every room had rough pine floors that were treated with linseed oil during the summer months. This created a problem when we returned to school in the fall. Many of the boys came to school barefooted, and the oil treatment caused splinters to stick straight up, and we got plenty of them in our feet. The school board finally installed a dark asphalt-like material over the rough pine, and that was the end of our splinters.

The authors' first day of school, Sept. 2, 1929

This school did not have inside plumbing. There was an outside toilet and a well for drinking water. At the beginning of the school year, each person was asked to bring a cup for drinking, which was to be kept in the coatroom. After the first few days, few of us would take the time to go to the coatroom to get our cup. Instead, we all drank from a community cup hanging from a wire on the pump. There were worms of some kind in the well one-year, and we could see them when we pumped a cup of water. The janitor came out and used baling wire to tie part of a cloth sack over the discharge of the pump so the worms would be filtered out.

The lawn of the schoolyard was Timothy Hay and it wouldn't be mowed until about a week before classes started. A local farmer with a team of horses and a mower would come and mow the yard. The boys would make big stacks out of the hay, and we would run and jump into them. We would continue this fun until the hay-stacks became too wet or rotten.

This old school building was connected with a rather unusual event in 1931. There were eight teachers in the Rochester school at this time, and the school board voted to fire all but one of them. The only one that was not fired was an older, single woman who taught first and second grade and was a native of Rochester. There was a scandal of some type going through the school and the school board decided this was the most appropriate action to take. I learned about this from my father, who was on the school board at the time. Such mass firings could never occur today because of tenure laws.

The eighth grade graduation exercises for all of the county schools were held at Springfield High during those years. The ceremony was a big event and may people came. I received the DAR award at this ceremony in 1937.

Most county high schools were three-year programs, with the fourth year at Springfield High School. A state law was passed allowing community four-year high-school programs. In 1936, Rochester needed a new building for its four-year high school and there was a big controversy over where it should be built. One potential site was the Howell Property north of town on what is now known as White Fence Acres. Another potential site was east of town on the highway to Buckhart, on what was called the McCoy Farm. This area is now a subdivision. The third area was a farm site, about ten acres in size, known as the Callerman farm. The Callerman site was chosen, and all of the houses and barns associated with their farm had to be torn down.

Work began on the new high school building and was to be completed by the fall of 1937. But for some reason, it was not ready when school started. Classes were held outside for two months. We sat on the grass, under the trees throughout the day. The school was finally finished in November, and we moved our classes inside. This new school was finished at a cost of $85,000.

The Rochester High School colors had been gold and purple. Since we had a new four-year high school, it was decided we needed new colors and a new nickname. "Orange and Blue" colors were selected and the nickname "Rockets" was adopted. It is a true story that Johnny Fields was the student who suggested the new school nickname. He had been reading Buck Rogers, and images of rockets were fresh in his mind.

I was elected to the school board in 1955, and became president in 1956. The main item before the board was the need for a new High School, Gymnasium and Cafeteria. However, some school board members did not believe that we could afford to build a new Gymnasium and Cafeteria, along with the new high school. I felt enough room should be allowed in the plans to build the new gym and cafeteria later. But, on a Friday afternoon, when the school board finished staking out the site for the new high school, room for the new gym and cafeteria was not allowed for. I went to the site by myself on the following Sunday and moved all of the stakes to the west, far enough to allow for the future construction of the new gym and cafeteria. Although everyone on the school board surely recognized that the stakes had been moved, no one said a word. Using the additional space made, the new gym and cafeteria was built a few years later.

The school board had greater control of the operation of the school when my dad and I were serving. We set salaries, and had a hand in most of the other operational duties of the school. I remember interviewing a prospective teacher who informed me that she had seventeen years of experience. I asked her if she had seventeen years of experience or one year of experience seventeen times. She was very upset over this question. When a teacher wanted to teach in the Rochester Schools, the school board, not the superintendent, selected them. The system is much different today.

In 1958 I decided not to seek reelection to the school board. I was township supervisor, and I learned that it was difficult to continue with the two jobs. I didn't serve as many years as my father, but I thought I had completed my duty.

As Rochester continued to expand, the school system continued to grow. We bought 300 feet of land on the north and west sides of the school in 1955. A new gym and cafeteria were built in 1960's and 1970 saw the construction of an addition to the high school. Twenty more acres of land were added during the 1970s, and 1800 students attended classes. A new elementary school was built in the 1990s, and an additional 200 acres of land were purchased. An all weather track was constructed at this time.

Rochester never had a football team until the 1990s. It seemed the cost was just too great. Then, a family donated $50,000 for the purchase of uniforms and equipment and Rochester has had a fine football team ever since.

Rochester Cemetery

The Rochester Cemetery is also associated with the Taft Family. The cemetery began in 1830 on the farm of my great grandfather William Taft. The first burial was a boy named Chris Stafford, who was the son of a family known to the Taft's from their days in Vermont.

In the early days of the burial ground, visitors had to go through William Taft's pasture, opening and closing gates to keep the livestock in. This site was used for burials for 25 years or more before the Taft's deeded five acres of their land into a trust for burial purposes. Munson Carter, C. B. Stafford, and Samuel B. Slater were named as trustees. All of these trustees had a connection to the Taft Family.

Another five acres of land just west of the initial tract was added to the burial grounds in 1855. Access continued to be through the pasture and barnyard of the Taft Farm. Pulling on a rope that had a 50-pound weight attached opened the gate. Once you passed through the gate, the rope could be pulled again and the gate would close. This system operated the gate from 1830 until 1920, a total of ninety years. I still have that 50-pound weight.

Ten more acres of land were purchased for the cemetery in 1920. During this same year a road was constructed to the cemetery. The road was built for horse and buggy travel plus early automobiles. This road was widened in the 1950s to accommodate more modern vehicles. A man named Mike Smith paid for this road improvement.

A chapel has built on the cemetery grounds in 1924. It was a good idea, but it was about 50 years too late. The increased use of automobiles made the chapel almost obsolete, and very few people use it today.

The ownership of the cemetery has changed since 1970, when the non-profit charter was given up after about 110 years. The property was turned over to the Rochester Township government and a tax levy is now implemented to pay for the upkeep of the cemetery.

Family traditions have changed and many families have moved away from Rochester. These changes made it impossible to depend on donations and gifts for maintenance of the cemetery. The township has done a very nice job of taking care of the cemetery that is the final resting place of many Rochester inhabitants.

History of Rochester Churches

The first organized religious meetings in Rochester took place in 1827 when some itinerant preachers would come and preach to the group that would be gathered in the local schoolhouse. Some of the early preachers were Methodist circuit riders that included Peter Cartwright from Pleasant Plains and another man named Cooper. Cooper Township takes its name from this man. Due to the influence of these circuit riders, Methodism was prevalent in Rochester Township, and there were four churches present in the early years. These churches were located in North Round Prairie, South Round Prairie, Rochester, and Forest Grove.

There is a brick building in Rochester on East Main Street, two houses east of the branch that has served as a residence for many, many years. However, its structure suggests that this building was once a church. No one remembers anything about it, but an old map of Rochester by Mr. Fred C. Tracy, has this building marked as a Universalist Church.

The first Methodist church in Rochester was built in 1842 on Back or Mill Street, as it is known today. This building was present in Rochester for many years. A Mr. McCoy, who was one of the founders of Rochester, was one of the leaders of this church. This church building served the congregation until 1924, a total of 82 years. They built a new brick church at the corner of North Walnut and Main Street in 1924, and it served the congregation until 2001 when they built a new church on South Walnut Street.

Original Methodist Church on E. Mill Street

During the early years, the people of the Christian Faith had been meeting in homes during cold weather, and in groves of timber during the summer. Some of the more influential families of this faith lived out in the country in the southern part of the township. In 1852 they built a meeting place just over the township line in Cotton Hill Township. It was near the South Fork River and was named the South Fork Christian Church. Most of the congregation that attended this church were from Rochester. After some time, the idea of building a church in Rochester developed, and a church was built in 1875. This building stood until 1917 when it was struck by lightning, causing the church to burn to the ground.

The congregation soon built another church on the same location. I attended this church and was baptized there in my youth. I attended Bible School their for many summers. A coal furnace heated this church, and one Sunday morning in February of 1947, sparks flew out of the chimney and started a small fire on the wooden shingles. Although a bucket of water could have put out the fire, no one had a ladder to get up on the roof. It wasn't long before the entire church was ablaze, causing it to burn to the ground. This tragedy caused the

Village of Rochester to think about the need for a fire department, which was soon developed. If anything good came out of this fire, it was the development of the fire department for protection of our buildings.

Another new church building was constructed on the same site. Three additions have been made to the original church, and the congregation has grown from approximately 60 members to over 600. Four services are held in the church each Sunday to accommodate the large number of members.

Christian Church the author first attended

For many years the Methodist and Christian Churches were the only two churches in Rochester. This started to change in the 1950s when Rochester's population grew from about 400 to over the current 3,000. A need for other churches developed during this period of rapid growth. The first new church was organized and built in about 1965 by the Lutherans. About 1980 the Catholic Church was built and named St. Jude's on South Walnut Street. The Baptists built a church on State Street about 1990, increasing the number of churches in Rochester to five.

The Characters Emerge

A Cast of Characters

There just doesn't seem to be any characters in town these days, but there were plenty in Rochester years ago. One of these characters was a woman named "Red Neer". She was an Irish woman that lived on Back Street (Mill Street). To high school boys like us, she seemed to be mad all of the time, and we used to say that her temper matched her red hair. We used to take advantage her short fuse as often as possible, especially on Halloween.

There was also a lady named Gussie May during the 1930s who was involved in politics. She was a firm believer in what was known as the Townsend plan, a federal proposal that would give every person in the country $200 if it passed the Congress and was signed into law by the president. She loved to talk about this plan, and would take any opportunity to explain it. When we saw her uptown, one of us would ask her to tell us about the Townsend proposal. She would start talking and a crowd would sometimes gather. The crowd would get her more excited, and she would keep on talking. The more excited she became, the louder she talked. Sometimes we kept her going for well over an hour. Despite her efforts, the Townsend proposal did not pass.

One of Rochester's most colorful characters was Frederick Steinhaur or "Steiny" as he was commonly known, and "Ding Bat" by his closest friends. He had his place of business in the basement of G.A. Wolford's hardware store. You could do many things at Steiny's place of business because Steiny was such a talented guy. He was the local Justice of the Peace, a Barber, repaired clocks, and had a Café known as the "Ding Bat Café", all in Wolford's basement. He charged 25 cents for a haircut and 15 cents for a shave. His skill at cleaning clocks consisted of rubbing the clock gears with a turkey feather soaked in kerosene. You could also get a sandwich and a bowl of chili. It was said that when you went to Steiny's shop, you could get something to eat, legal advice, solve legal arguments, get a shave and haircut all in one stop. Sadly, the hardware store burned in 1930, and Steiny had to start a new shop in the rear of the Odd Fellows Lodge where he operated his shop until about 1985.

When Steiny's shop was in the basement of the hardware store, the only windows were in the front and opened out onto the sidewalk, at sidewalk level. During the summer months, these windows were open in order to get good ventilation for his customers. The windows were hinged at the top, and hooked to the ceiling. His combs and clippers were kept on a table just below the windows. The barber chairs were next to this table. Some of the local boys thought of a fine trick on Steiny. They gathered some dog urine and put it on the screen covering the barbershop windows. When the windows were open, and a local dog came by, he was likely to cock his leg on Steiny's screen and dampen the clippers, combs, or customer. This would cause an awful commotion in the barbershop, with much yelling and cussing of the dog.

Nearly every barbershop had spittoons in those days, and his was no exception. However, he had a rather unusual use for the hair he swept up. When he cleaned up hair from the floor, he put some of it in each of the spittoons. The small amount of hair kept the tobacco from splashing when customers would spit into them.

"Steiny" had some unusual habits. He was cutting my cousin Ben Taft's hair one morning before school had started, when the whistle of the passenger train sounded at 9:00 AM. Steiny had finished just one side of his haircut, and he said that he had to go into Springfield on the train. He told Ben to "come back in the morning and I'll finish the other side of your head" as he dashed out the door to get on the train.

"Steiny" also had an unusual way to determine his age in later years.

He proudly stated that he was 85 years old, but after two months he would be 87. When two more months passed, he would say that he was 89. He wanted to live to be 100, so the months seemed to get changed into years. He had developed a new system of aging.

Sign directing customers to Steiny's shop below Wolford's hardware store

It was easy to see Steiny was never one to turn away an opportunity to make money. One evening, just 10 minutes before he was to close, I was waiting to take him to the Buckhart Tavern when a woman brought four little boys in for haircuts. They were all walking out the door with their mother ten minutes later, and he had his money. It seems that he wanted to make sure that he got to the Buckhart tavern on time, and what do they expect for $.25 a haircut?

31

You could also find several characters sitting on what was called the "liar's bench" at the grocery store at "Uptown" Rochester. They always had a story to tell and they knew about all of the events happening in town, good or bad. One of these guys was a man that had worked for us for a few days. He was talking about the good chicken dinner he had eaten recently at our house while he was working for us. A few weeks later a thunderstorm with lots of lightning came through the area. The alarm bell on our chicken house sounded. During one lightning flash, my dad saw a man running from the chicken house, and he insisted it was the same man that had worked for us a few weeks earlier and had been bragging about the fine chickens that we raised.

Without naming names, four Rochester gentlemen went to Springfield one evening and attended a few taverns. They all ended up at the "Golden Gate" tavern, north of the fairgrounds. This tavern stayed open all night and even cooked breakfast for them. They returned to Rochester at about 8 o'clock the next morning. One of the gentlemen who lived at home with his mother was asked, "Where in the world have you been"? He replied that he had been to the movies. She asked: "What movie did you see?" His reply was "Tom Mix and Tony Went Wild". Of course, no such movie was ever produced. This is but one of many capers in which these characters were involved. This gives a bad image of the Rochester "Gentry", but some activity like this went on at least twice a week.

There were two St. Clair brothers in town in the 1930s. They bought a large touring car and took turns driving it around town. The only unusual thing about this activity was that one would dress nicely and wear a chauffeur's cap while the other brother rode in the back seat. Everyone that knew these two brothers believed that they were just trying to make some people believe that a chauffeur was driving them.

The Rochester vicinity also had its share of individuals that would much rather steal than work to make a living. One such character, upon being found guilty of stealing a hog, had been sentenced to serve time in prison. Our county sheriff, who had just bought two new white shirts, was to take him to Vandalia where he was to serve his sentence. When the sheriff returned to his office, he noticed that his prisoner had stolen one of his new shirts. The convicted man apparently wanted something nice to wear while he served his time.

No mention of characters would be complete without the Dawley brothers. They lived together in one of the last log homes in the Rochester vicinity. They did farm work now and then, but they were more inclined to not work if they could get by any other way. They liked to hunt and usually had a few coon dogs with them in their house. They had only one bed, and usually slept together, especially during winter. They also brought their dogs inside during the cold weather, and the dogs often slept under the blankets with them.

Dawley brothers, Bill and Brady with a favorite hound dog

One of the Dawley Brothers favorite pastimes was making home brew. They kept their brew cool in the summer by putting it in a burlap bag and lowering it into the well with baling wire. I went to their well one summer day with my pony and cart to fill jugs of water for a threshing crew. When I arrived at the well, I discovered their bag of home brew. Instead of lowering it gently back into the well, I tossed it down. I soon heard the sound of breaking glass. When I returned to the threshing, the men said there was a bad taste in the water that I had brought back to them.

There was another man in town that talked about the jobs that he had in his life. He would talk about working for the railroad, raising purebred hogs, operating a dairy farm, and working as a carpenter. If you added all of the years he worked in each of these occupations, he would have been over 120 years old.

There was also a man is town that was the local tinsmith. His name was Hoopie Smith, and he usually worked about one day out of the week. This would earn him a little money, and he would buy some whiskey and be drunk the rest of the week. He did good work when he was sober. Hoopie was the person that made the copper boiler we used to make Suet pudding. He also repaired a leak in the roof of the Capitol building while it was being built.

There were those on the liar's bench in those days that knew all about digging wells by hand. Some of these individuals had never had a steady job, but they managed to make ends meet somehow. They would dig a well, and line it with bricks. Most of the wells they dug did not go beyond 25 feet in depth. They knew how to use dynamite and used it to blast out rock. They were also good at what was called jugging. This was the term used when they had to make the top narrower than the lower part of the well. The end result was a well that had the shape of a jug. This could be necessary in some soil types.

Many of them would not attempt to dig a well unless the site had been witched. One of the favorite woods for witching was peach. The usual procedure was to find a young, forked peach branch. The person doing the witching held on to the ends of the forks and walked holding the branch horizontally. When the branch bent down toward the ground, water was present. Some of the individuals that did the "witching" would say the branch turned so hard it hurt their hands.

The same men that dug wells were also good at digging and laying field tiles. They could dig the tile line and lay the tile without the benefit of a level or a surveyor's transit. These old timers simply used a glass jug of water. It was remarkable they could complete the work with such simple tools.

There was a landowner named Paul Krider from Springfield who owned a 160-acre farm east of Rochester. When his tenant farmer left, he had to find another person to farm the land. One of the stipulations made to all of the potential new tenants was that they would be required to put a fish in every hill of corn they planted each spring. No one would agree to put a fish in all of the hills of corn on a 160-acre farm, so no new tenant was found. Trees quickly grew up on the farm and it was no longer useable. When the landowner passed away, all of the brush and small trees were cleared away and the land was farmed again.

Big Charlie Fairchild and the Bear

Charlie Fairchild, who was known as "Big Charlie", ran a butcher market in what now is the"Town Hall", located next to the school in Rochester. Around 1910, he had a black bear he kept chained to a tree behind the butcher shop. No one knows exactly how he managed to find a bear, but he had one. The bones and meat left from the butchering were given to the bear. The bear had plenty to eat and was getting pretty big.

As can be imagined, the bear was quite an attraction. People came by Big Charlie's shop with the sole intention of looking at the bear. It was a bonus to Big Charlie if they went inside his shop to buy meat.

Big Charlie came up with the idea of killing the fattened bear and having a big party in the fall once the corn had been shucked. I don't know why he waited until that time unless he wanted to make sure everyone could come to his party. The main course for dinner at his party was going to be bear meat.

The Town Hall was built by "Big Charlie Fairchild" as a meat market

True to his word, Big Charlie killed the bear after the corn was harvested and a big crowd went to his party in Springfield. My uncle's 38-40 caliber, single shot rifle was used to kill the bear, and the meat was roasted over an open fire. This was likely the last bear to visit Rochester, tame or not.

Big Charlie's party was held in a saloon in Springfield, and playing cards were one of the main activities besides drinking. It wasn't long before most of the men were pretty drunk and some arguments took place about the card games. Big Charlie was involved, and the drinking had triggered his volatile temper. Suddenly, Big Charlie pulled out a pistol from his pocket and shot Alvey Miller's hired man. The man fell to the floor and soon died from his wound.

Big Charlie was now in serious trouble with the law. He had to sell his meat market to pay his lawyers, who were successful during the trial at gaining his freedom. He moved to Kansas after the trial and was never seen again in Rochester.

The bear party resulted in one man's death, a costly trial and the ultimate departure of Big Charlie from Rochester. Maybe it is a good thing Rochester has seen no black bear's since the last one was barbequed.

Hoover's Headquarters

Mr. Oliver, the man who owned and operated Oliver's Clover Farm grocery in Rochester, was a staunch Republican. In fact, Mr. Oliver was about the only Republican in town at this time. Political tension was running high in Rochester in 1932 when Franklin D. Roosevelt and Herbert Hoover were running for president. Being the only Republican in town was not an easy life.

Many of the high school boys knew about Mr. Oliver's strong support for Republicans. When Halloween came around they managed to move a large outhouse under the porch of his store, close to the front entrance. Then they put a large sign on it that read: "Hoover's Headquarters." It sat there for a week and was the talk of the town. It was also the source of much laughter and many jokes.

The situation with the outdoor toilet was made worse by the fact that Mr. Oliver's store was also the local post office at the time. Many people came there to send or pick up their mail, and all of them left laughing about "Hoover's Headquarters." Mr. Oliver breathed a sigh of relief when he finally got the boys to carry it away from his store.

Halloween Capers

Halloween was a great and fun event in Rochester when I was a young boy. We didn't wait until Halloween actually arrived like other boys. We started doing tricks a month ahead of time. We often did not ask anyone "Trick or treat." We just did the tricks. It was a lot more fun that way.

Everyone had an outhouse in those days, and it was a common Halloween prank to turn these over. There were windows to be soaped, corn fodder to be thrown on porches, dogs to be turpentined, or wagons to be put on top of the school house. There were plenty of activities to keep us busy.

As I look back on my youth I think about how simple it was then. We didn't have police to chase us. We had just a few irate homeowners that couldn't take a joke to contend with in those years. Some of these would yell at us or fire a shotgun into the air.

One of my favorite stories involves a man who bragged that no one could upset his outhouse. He had it secured with heavy number nine wire at each corner. We went to his house late one night and used wire cutters to cut the supports. His outhouse ended up on the ground like the rest of them.

Another story involves a group of boy's in a pick-up truck who had been driving around Rochester throwing corn fodder on select home owners front porch's. This was so much fun that this group had been doing this for the last three nights. This pick-up was loaded with boys, including the cab, rear bed area and two boys laying on the front fenders. As they approached a selected house for the third straight night, the owner came out with a shotgun and blew out the front tire of the pickup truck. One boy that was on the front fender of the truck was glad that the man was a good shot. We had the tire repaired at the local service station and we dumped forty-two pellets out of the old tire. The man that shot the tire was the local Methodist preacher.

One of my favorite Halloween pranks was a practice that we called tick tacking. All that was needed for this trick was a long, thin knife and a long piece of sturdy string. It was important that the knife was thin, but also strong so it would assume its original shape after being bent, much like a saw blade. We would sneak up to a house, push the end of the knife up under the boards, and tie the string to the end of the knife. Then we would unroll the string until we were at a place where we could hide. Then we would pull the string tight and pluck it like a guitar string. The knife would vibrate and cause a noise that sounded like a storm was coming. People would run out of their houses to see what was happening. Others knew what was going on and came out of their houses with a shotgun, and sometimes fired a few shots into the air. We pulled this trick on "Red" Neer once, and she didn't appreciate it very much. She came running out of her house, holding a butcher knife in her hand, and started chasing us. We took off running as fast as we could go. We tried to distract her by running into a Fowler's restaurant, but she came in after us, still clutching that knife. We ran toward the back, through their kitchen, and out the back door, and she never stopped chasing us with that knife. I guess we finally wore her out because she stopped chasing us not long after going through the restaurant. I was glad that she stopped. The sight of that butcher knife was starting to worry me.

Another great Halloween trick that was one of my favorites was putting farm wagons up on the schoolhouse roof. Remember that farm wagons were readily available in those days, so finding one was no problem. We would find one as close to the school as possible and push in to the school grounds where it would be disassembled. One of us would climb up the gutter to get on the schoolhouse roof with a rope. Then, he would pull each part of the wagon up, where it was reassembled. The owner generally knew where to find his missing wagon. The hardest part for the owner was getting the wagon off the roof. One of the worst stories I heard was about a wagon that was put on the roof of a grain elevator in Dawson, Illinois, a small town north of Rochester. One of the boys that miraculously got the wagon on the elevator was standing around admiring his work the next morning when the wagon owner approached him. The wagon owner didn't know the boy was involved and asked him if he could get the wagon down for five dollars. The boy said he sure could, took the five dollars, and proceeded to the elevator roof where he kicked the chocks out from under the wheels and let the wagon roll off the roof. He didn't know how much damage was done to the wagon, but it was off the elevator roof and he had his five dollars.

Approaching Storm

Anyone that knew Uncle Henry Taft was aware that all work done on his farm had to be absolutely perfect. If it wasn't, he was sure to let you know about it. That also meant every available minute should be spent working. Anything resembling idle time would not be tolerated. If grain was spilled or someone was sitting for a while, he would be sure to start yelling at the offending person.

Henry Taft's house as it appeared in 1917

Jim Drillinger was one of Uncle Henry's hired hands. He was a good worker, but he was sort of a hothead himself. Born in 1863, he had worked for the Taft family all of his life. There was never any question about the quality of his work or his dedication to the Taft farm.

Jim had been cultivating corn all morning and at noon, took the horses to the barn to feed them. He returned to wash up before eating lunch. It was the custom in those days for all of the farm workers to have lunch with the farm family in the farm home. When Jim finished eating, he went outside to return to cultivating corn. That's when he noticed a big thunderstorm approaching from the west.

With the chance of rain, cultivating crops was not on his mind any longer. Instead of going to the barn to get the horses, Jim went to sleep under a shade tree in the yard. Uncle Henry came outside and found Jim sleeping soundly. He woke him up and wanted to know why he wasn't cultivating. Jim replied that a storm was coming and it would soon be raining. That didn't make a bit of difference to Uncle Henry. He shouted to Jim to: "Get out there and get to work! I will tell you when to work and when to quit."

Jim got the horses, hitched them to cultivators and went to the field to cultivate corn. It started to rain when Jim got to the far end of the field. When it started to rain more, Jim didn't stop working. He took off his shoes, tied them to the cultivator, and kept cultivating corn despite the downpour. Water was running down the field behind the cultivator. Uncle Henry watched him, but did nothing for a long time.

When the rain stopped, he went to the field and told Jim to stop. "Don't you know that you will ruin the crop if you don't stop cultivating in this rain and mud? Why didn't you stop when it started to rain"? Jim replied: "You told me that you would tell me when it was going to rain. You never came out, so I kept cultivating the corn." Uncle Henry never questioned Jim again when he stopped work as a storm was approaching.

Justin Taft

The "House of Mystery"

Many people have asked me what I know about those "frame buildings in bad repair" at Hill Top and Route 29. I know that one of them was built to be a "Road House" or "Tavern", as we would call it now. In 1932, Prohibition was voted out, making Rochester a wet township. In other words, liquor could be sold legally. As a matter of fact, the entire country was wet due to the repeal of Prohibition. I believe a man by the name of Frank Kluzek built these buildings intending to go into the tavern business, believing it was a sure way of getting rich.

Frank had many friends on the east side of Springfield that came to his tavern plus those from Rochester. I believe he had a very good business whose name endures to this day. He painted a sign on the west side of his tavern calling his place "House of Mystery". Underneath this sign was a painting of a scantly clad lady. No one knows why the tavern was given this name, but it caused many individuals to wonder what activities were taking place in the building. I never heard any stories of bad behavior, but it was out in the country and no one lived close by to complain if they stayed open late or got a little rowdy.

What I remember most about the "House of Mystery" involved our "ice man." He stopped there every afternoon and stayed for several hours, causing our 50-pound block of ice to melt down to about 40 pounds by the time he made his delivery to our home. After drinking for several hours, I am not sure that he could tell what the ice blocks weighed. Many people in Rochester also made the same complaint to him.

I believe the tavern caused concerns for our local folks, particularly, the Rochester town fathers. They wanted to ban the sale of all alcoholic beverages. I guess they thought Prohibition had worked pretty well for the residents. They knew that the state constitution provided for "Local Options" on such matters, but they had to be voted on by the residents. Elections were held every four years, so the town fathers

42

had to wait till 1936 to vote on the "Local Option". In the mean time, the "House of Mystery" had a good four-year run. The good times came to an end in 1936 for the "House" when the township was voted dry. It has been dry ever since.

This is what's left of the Front Entrance to the "House of Mystery"
P.S. As we go to Press the House of Mystery is Demolished Jan 2004

We were still in the Great Depression when the "House of Mystery" had to close. People, looking for a cheap home, moved into the abandoned tavern building and it served as a home for many years. Several of the other buildings were built after this time. Lack of maintenance caused the building to fall into disrepair until even the poorest and most needy families would not live there. No one has lived in the place since 1980 and the building is in considerable disrepair. Until "Father Time" collapses the old buildings, we will still be looking at the old weathered boards and sagging roofs. Despite their condition and the passing of over 70 years, people are still wondering what took place in "The House of Mystery."

Adventures Along the South Fork

The Cabin

The big project for us during the summer of 1933 was the construction of a cabin on the Taft property not far from the South Fork of the Sangamon River. My cousin Ernest, my brother Bill and I got the idea from a story we had read about a family from Maine who built a cabin in the woods. After reading that story, we thought about a cabin and had an idea on how we could build one. It was a big job for us. My cousin Ernest was 13, brother Bill was 12 and I was 9 years old at the time.

The author "sawing wood", Ernest in middle and brother Bill, on right

We found a cross cut saw and started cutting down trees to use in making the walls. Most of the trees we cut were Honey Locusts, and we selected those that had straight trunks and were about eight inches in diameter. The logs were pretty heavy, so we used our ponies, Teddy and Spot, to pull the logs to the cabin site.

We made sure all of the locust thorns were cut off the logs before hitching them to the ponies. We were also extra careful to watch the ponies so they did not step on any of the thorns. We tied them to trees at the end of the day, and they would eat the grass that was nearby. They stayed there all night and never seemed to mind being outside. We did worry about them one night when a thunderstorm with lots of lightning came through the Rochester area.

We didn't use any nails in the cabin's construction, so all logs had to be carefully measured and notched to fit properly. We used a small hatchet to notch the logs before they were put in place. We didn't square any logs, so we sometimes had gaps an inch wide in the walls. We filled the gaps with a mixture of clay and grass mud. This was the method described in the book.

No cabin would be complete without a fireplace for heat and cooking. We were fortunate to get all the bricks we wanted from the demolished old jail in Rochester. It was a job transporting all of those bricks to the cabin site. We loaded them on a farm wagon and hauled them to the construction site using our team of horses. But, there was an even bigger job. We needed sand to make the mortar for building the fireplace. The nearest sand was along the river about a half-mile away. We had to make lots of trips to that sand bar and carry five-gallon buckets back to the cabin. It was a long, hard walk with those buckets of sand.

The only part of the construction that gave us trouble was the roof. We couldn't figure out how to make a V-shaped roof like the ones you see on most log cabins, so we made a sloping roof, and it worked just fine. When we finished construction in January of 1933, we were pretty proud of our accomplishment.

We did all of our cooking on the fireplace, using a cast iron skillet and pot. We fixed mush, ham, bacon and fried eggs in the skillet. We baked potatoes by wrapping them in newspaper, covering them with mud and tossing them into the fire. They had a little bit of a mud taste, but we didn't care. The cast iron pot was used to make chili that we ate for dinner.

We never threw chili away. We ate any leftovers for breakfast. When the chili tasted a little funny one morning, we discovered a chunk of mud had fallen into the pot. We had mixed it in and had eaten it by mistake for breakfast. We were more careful after that. We didn't want to eat any more mud.

The furnishings of the cabin contained only what we needed, including a table, two wooden chairs and a bed. We had a dirt floor, and there were no windows. We cut plenty of wood for the fireplace and it supplied the light most of the time. The fireplace proved to be a good place to cook our food.

The cabin stayed plenty warm during the winter months when we had a good fire going. We continued to use it for ten years. There was plenty to keep us busy, including cutting wood, fishing, and swimming. During the autumn and winter, we set a few traps along the river to try to catch coons and muskrats. Our trapping was never very profitable.

As we grew older, we began to lose interest in the cabin and did not use it nearly as much. A hired man of ours named Jim, thought it would be a good place to live, and moved in. He installed a pot-bellied stove for heating and cooking. Jim lived in it for about two years. He taught us how to make snares to catch rabbits. He often had a ½ gallon syrup can with a rabbit in it, boiling on the old stove.

Jim was living in our cabin when it was lost during the big flood of 1943. This was no annual flood; but is still the biggest flood known to have ever occurred on the South Fork of the Sangamon River. Our cabin had lasted ten years and we were sad to lose it. Jim moved out as the water rose higher. We never tried to build another cabin, but we were sure proud of the one we built in the summer of 1933. We had a lot of fun moments and the cabin left us with memories that have lasted a lifetime.

Coon Hunting

My brother, cousin, and I spent many weekend nights in the cabin that we built near the South Fork River. Most nights were pretty uneventful. We spent the evenings cooking and eating chili that we made in an iron pot that rested on a grate, set over the fire. We talked for hours, and kept the fire going throughout the night.

We were there one autumn night when we kept hearing the sound of hunting dogs. It sounded like they were on our property, and they were pretty close to the cabin. We were curious, and wanted to know what was happening, so we took off into the darkness to locate the source of the noise. It wasn't long before we saw a flashlight in the distance, so we slowly moved towards it. I was walking along very cautiously in the dark when a man grabbed me and held me in a tight grip.

"What are you boys doing?" he asked in a gruff voice. "Are you trying to steal my dogs?" We explained that we were staying in a nearby cabin and we had heard the dogs, but we weren't trying to steal any of them. There had been quite a bit of dog stealing going on in recent weeks, so we could see why he was suspicious of us.

Then we asked him why he was on our land without permission. He changed his tone of voice a bit after this question, and he mellowed considerably when he learned that he was talking to the sons of the landowner. We were so scared of him that we didn't say anything more. We were glad to get away from him and get back to the cabin. We never saw him or heard his dogs again, despite all the nights that we spent in the cabin. Even if we had heard dogs, I doubt that we would have gone to see who was there. That one experience of being grabbed in the dark was enough for us.

None of us went coon hunting by ourselves, but I did go later when

I was operating the farm. People would come and ask permission to hunt, and I would sometimes give them permission on the condition that I would go with them. I remember one night when I was on our farm with a coon hunter. We could hear one of his dogs in the distance, and the coon hunter said: "Old Blue has a coon up a tree." We walked to the barking sound and soon found the dog. He didn't have a coon up a tree. "Old Blue" was stuck in a field tile and couldn't get out. He had followed a coon into an open ten-inch field tile and could not back out.

We had no alternative but to dig a hole down to the tile, where we thought the dog was. We could only see him by shining a flashlight down the tile. We estimated that he was about 30 feet in. We went back to the barn and got spades and shovels, and started digging. We knew he wouldn't back up, so we started digging ahead of where we thought he was. It was a deep hole. The tile was some four feet in the ground. We finally got down to where the tile was and removed two tiles. We called him to come to us, and he jumped right out. I was never so happy to see an old coon-hound. Then, we had to put the tiles back and fill in the hole we had dug. What a way to spend the night.

I didn't get back home until 2:00 in the morning. I never went coon hunting again.

Visit from the "Gypsies"

In the spring of 1933 during Easter vacation, we were at our log cabin when two big black Packard touring cars came slowly down the path from the highway. I have no idea how they knew we were there unless they could see us from the highway. They stopped at the cabin, and three men and two women got out of the cars. All of them had dark complexions and the men were wearing hats and long dark coats. The men walked over to us and began to talk. We didn't know them and they never mentioned their names.

We did know that we were afraid of them. This was an era of gangsters, and we thought they had come to Rochester. One of them said that they wanted some wood to roast a goat for Easter. We knew these people were not from the Rochester area. We did not know of any family that roasted a goat for Easter. We thought they were from a city far from this area. This thought only increased our fear of them. We eagerly filled the trunks of their cars with wood, hoping that they would get back inside and drive away. Then we would be rid of them.

We had worked the entire day cutting that wood, but we were glad to give it to them. Fortunately, they left as soon as the wood was loaded. They now had the wood they needed to roast their goat, but the wood that we had worked so hard to cut was gone in a matter of minutes. It was nice oak wood that we had split for use in our fireplace. Now we didn't have any for ourselves. The worst part was that they left without offering to pay anything for the wood. We didn't care. We thought that they could have put *us* in the trunks of those big cars and hauled us off like they were taking the wood. Their big black cars and long black coats had scared us quite a bit. We were glad to see them leave. As we began to relax, we started calling them "Gypsies". We were never sure who they were or where they were from. We never saw them again, and we were glad of that. It was an experience that we didn't want to repeat.

Maple Syrup Time

Recently, I visited Lincoln Memorial Garden at Lake Springfield. The process of making maple syrup was being demonstrated. Maple sap was being cooked down in a large metal trough over an open fire. I enjoyed watching the process because it reminded me of the spring season of 1935 when my dad told me about the Taft Family tradition of making maple syrup. That tradition went back to his grandfather who brought it to Rochester from Vermont. My dad made syrup every spring at the "Sugar Camp", which was located near the South Fork River on Taft family land. This tradition probably started shortly after the Civil War, and continued to about 1920, when the "Sugar Camp" was destroyed by fire. It was never rebuilt. I remember going to this site with my dad and seeing the bricks, which were used to hold the four-foot long, three-foot wide cast iron trough. A fire was started under this trough and the maple sap was boiled down to make syrup. It is likely that the syrup was sold or traded for items that were needed.

That day at Lincoln Memorial Gardens brought back memories from the spring of 1935. It was this spring that my bother Bill, my cousin Ernest Taft and I were allowed to stay out of school for a week in order to make maple syrup. We tapped about ten maple trees that grew on our property. We used a one-inch drill bit and drilled a hole in the trees about two feet above the ground. We prepared spouts from Sumac trees to put in the hole of the Maple tree so the sap would run into our buckets. Small limbs were cut from Sumac trees and the soft inner core was punched out to make them hollow. This made a perfect spout.

Maple trees will produce about ten gallons of sap each. This sap runs from the roots of the tree to the upper branches each spring, starting about February 8th through the first of March. We had two large cast iron kettles. As we gathered the sap in the buckets, we carried it to these large kettles, under which we had a hot fire. We added the sap daily to the kettles. It was a big job to cut enough firewood to keep a hot fire going 24 hours a day, but this had to be done. This was the only way to cook the sap down enough. It generally takes about 40 gallons of sap to make one gallon of syrup.

Ernest, my brother Bill and I busied ourselves for the week we were out of school, collecting sap in our buckets and keeping the fire going. We had the fire and cooking process located just outside our log cabin. We three boys had built this cabin in the winter of 1933. We had an open fireplace in the cabin to keep us warm and to cook on. So you can see, we were very busy cutting wood and tending the kettles. We slept in shifts so that someone was always awake to care for the fires.

As you can see, this was all work and no play. As the week came to an end and school was to be attended next week, we prepared to stop our operation. We stopped collecting the sap from the trees and finished cooking down the sap in the kettles. On Sunday afternoon, we were happy to pour the maple syrup from our week's work in a three-gallon cream can, put the fires out and start our long walk home. Our parents were happy to see us and glad to have some nice maple syrup to put on our pancakes.

Paw Paws, Persimmons, and Red Haws

It was a tradition in my family to go to the woods every late summer or early fall to gather Paw-Paws. We would walk down to the woods and find areas where the ground was moist. The Paw-Paws would be growing in shade underneath the larger Oaks, Hickories and Maples. Paw Paws have the habit of forming a dense patch, and once one gets started from seed, others will develop from the roots until a Paw-Paw patch is formed.

Paw-Paws never develop into very big trees, and it is rare to find one that is more than five or six inches in diameter. They have long, wide leaves and are borne alternately along their limber branches. They bloom early in the spring, and the dark brown blooms develop into a fruit that is shaped like a medium-sized potato, but the outside is smooth and light green in color. The inside of the fruit, when ripe, is yellow and it contains many large brown seeds. Some say that this fruit has the flavor of custard, but there is little flesh left once the seeds have been removed.

We usually took a sack along when we went to gather Paw-Paws. We could see them hanging from the upper branches, just out of reach. Most trees were small enough to allow us to shake them to make the fruits fall to the ground. The trees would not have fruits on them every year, but we were generally not disappointed.

We managed to fill a small sack with paw paws each fall, and we brought these back to our home. We would peel the Paw-Paws and eat them like a Banana. My grandfather liked Paw-Paws, and when he was too old to walk very far, he would ask us each fall to go to the woods to get some for him to eat. We used the Paw-Paws just for eating; we didn't make any desserts or any other type of food out of them.

We had several Persimmon trees on our farm and we would pick the Persimmons when they were ripe, following the first frosts. Our mother would use some of them to make cookies, and we would eat a few of them. They had lots of seeds in them that were about the same size as the seeds in the Paw-Paws. If there was a "Green-Horn" around, we would give him a Persimmon that was not quite ripe. These were not quite as soft and had a slight green color to them and they were also extremely bitter. They would pucker their mouths and run for water.

We also liked to ride our ponies down into the pasture where we would find the Red Haws. They were one of the Hawthorns that produced an apple like fruit, about the size of a quarter. They were tart and fun to eat, and we gathered them in sacks and brought them back to eat. If we managed to get enough, our mother would make Red Haw jelly. It had a good flavor, and we enjoyed the small amount that she made.

Picking Paw-Paws, Persimmons, and Red Haws is something that few people do today, but I have many fond memories of picking and eating these fruits. It was a ritual for us when we were kids.

Hogging for Fish

Hogging was a name given to catching fish by hand in creeks or small rivers. This activity usually took place during summer, when the water levels had dropped low enough to allow individuals to wade through most parts of the stream. During this time of the year, big fish, such as catfish, were often stranded in the deeper pools and were often unable to get back to bigger bodies of water.

People of all ages were involved in this activity. The trick to the "hogging" was to find a fish in a logjam and slowly move your hands up to the gills where it was possible to get a firm hold on the fish. This was particularly important because they would put up a big fight, and several of them would manage to get away despite all efforts to hold them securely.

The ultimate object of all of this activity was a big fish fry. There was a lot of work to be done with preparing the fish. There were two or three people cleaning the fish, others were dipping the fish in corn meal batter and three or four people were frying the fish.

Most of the hogging in the Rochester area took place in the South Fork River. Most of the fish we hogged in this stream were catfish or carp, but buffalo were also caught. The excitement rose when a big catfish would be found in one of the logjams. It was always interesting to see how much of a struggle the men would have in the water with the fish.

There were some individuals that were especially good at hogging. Norman Braner and Lester Hobbs always seemed to know where to search and how to catch fish. Others watched these men closely when they were hogging, hoping they could learn the secrets of their success.

Most everyone had a job when hogging fish. I liked to carry the sack and pick up the fish that were tossed up onto the bank. It didn't take long before the sack started to get pretty heavy, especially if I had picked up a few large carp or buffalo.

There was one man in town that always got more fish while hogging than anyone else. His success attracted the attention of the local game warden that wanted to know why he was so successful. The two arranged to go hogging one day, and the warden soon got his answer. The man got into a boat with the game warden and went to a deep pool of water. He took a stick of dynamite from a sack, lit the fuse, and handed it to the warden. The warden said, "You can't do that, it's illegal". The "fish hogger" said, "Are you going to debate the law or fish". As the fuse got shorter and shorter, the warden had no choice but to throw it into the water. There was a tremendous explosion underwater, and it wasn't long before all sorts of fish were floating on the surface. No arrests were made because the game warden threw the dynamite into the water. He was an accomplice to the illegal activity. It is most likely that was the last time the game warden went hogging with this fisherman.

There were always more people at the fish fry than at the hogging or cleaning of the fish. Most everyone liked to eat fried fish, especially if they had a fresh jug of beer to drink. Rochester was dry, but beer could be purchased in Springfield. The taverns would fill a clear glass jug with beer for a dollar. Many people would show up at the fish fry with their jugs and they would be passed around to those that did not have any beer. Sometimes twenty people would drink out of the same jug of beer.

There usually were no games or music at these fish fry's. There were plenty of stories being told about the big one that got away, or the struggle one man had to catch a big catfish. There were also plenty of lies being told, so there was no need for any other type of entertainment.

Glenwood Amusement Park

Few individuals would ever believe that there once was an amusement park on the South Fork River approximately three miles north of Rochester. This park was started about 1890 when a dam was placed across the river to increase the water level so a steamboat could carry passengers to and from the park. The dam raised the water level of the South Fork about six feet.

Steamship on the South Fork near "Glenwood Park"

This steamboat was not large, nor did it resemble the Delta Queen or Titanic. It was about the size of the steamboat used in the classic movie "The African Queen." Humphrey Bogart would have been at home in this steamboat that carried passengers to Glenwood Park. The steamboat would also dock at the B & O tracks and pick up passengers for a day of fun.

The Springfield, Clear Lake, and Rochester Railway also provided transportation to this park. Railroad personnel hoped to profit from the large number of people attracted to the recreational facilities at both Glenwood Park and Clear Lake.

Glenwood Park "Pavilion" in its latter days

The park had quite a few attractions, including a bowling alley, dance hall, roller coaster, covered bridge, and restaurant. Big crowds were attracted to the site from 1890 to about 1910. It was getting expensive to maintain after this time, and the owners closed it at the end of the summer.

All of the buildings are gone and it would not be possible to find any part of the old amusement park. The only reminder of the park is a small portion of the dam immediately above where Black Branch enters the South Fork. The dam was broken when the park closed.

I am not sure what happened to the steamboat, but I suspect that it was junked like the other parts of the park. I do know that my dad had the opportunity to ride on it several times before the park closed. There was very little left of the park by 1915.

There was a large outcropping of sandstone on the South Fork not far from Glenwood Park that we called "Starved Rock." This rock was larger than most houses, and stood about 75 feet above the river. We often camped there and hiked through the woods long after the disappearance of Glenwood Park. The river had cut into this rock over the years and we were able to ride our ponies under the overhang when the water was low. Starved Rock was also changed a few years ago when a house was built on its top. Starved Rock was not far from Gobbler's Knob, the site of the tavern and dance hall.

The Old Swimming Hole

There were no swimming pools in the 1930s and 1940s in Rochester or the surrounding area. Younger people had no way of getting to Springfield where there was a public pool. The only other way to keep cool during the hot summer months was to find a swimming hole.

Our favorite place to swim was a deep hole in the South Fork River. Some people thought this river was way too muddy for swimming, but I used to say that the muddy water made it easier to swim. There was more resistance with the muddy water compared to clear water. I am not sure I convinced many people.

We usually did not go swimming during the hottest part of the day. We would wait until the chores were done in the evening and then we would walk along the railroad tracks to the river. Getting to the tracks wasn't the easiest thing to do because of the steep bank above the tracks. We would cut steps into the clay bank with a spade so we could get down to the tracks. Then, we would walk the rails down to the river. Now the railroad and the tracks are gone, replaced by a bike path. Nice concrete steps have also been built into the bank where we used to slide down. I like to tell people that those nice new steps were built for me after my 75th birthday so I could get down to the new bicycle path.

We also had to go down a rather steep bank to get to the water once we got to the river. If it had rained recently, that bank was often very slick. Sometimes we would use a spade to cut steps in the bank so we wouldn't slip. This helped us for most of the summer, but they were usually gone by the next year, and sometimes a gully formed where they had been located.

The pool we used for swimming was not the deepest place around, but it did have a hard, yellow clay bottom on one side that was ideal for getting in and out of the river. Since most of the river had mud banks, this proved to be very helpful. We found this clay spot by accident. Since we swam in our birthday suits, we didn't want to climb out of the water through mud on the bank to get to our clothes.

My brothers and I decided to build a diving platform one summer. We got some rough-sawed cottonwood lumber and started to build our platform. It looked pretty good, and we were expecting to have lots of fun diving into the water.

When we finally finished, one of the neighbor boys decided to take the first jump into the water. After walking out a few feet onto the platform, we heard a loud crack and the platform and boy fell into the river. We realized our mistake was using cottonwood lumber. It was much too brittle to hold any of us. That summer was our one and only attempt at making a diving platform at the river.

We made our hike to the river and swam practically every evening during the summer months. Some of us even went swimming when the river was flooded. During these times it wasn't possible to swim against or across the current. We had to let the water carry us downstream until we found a place where we could get out. When I reflect upon those days, swimming during the floods may have been much too dangerous, but none of us had any problems.

The floods also brought some unwelcome changes in water quality. About three days after a flood, the water would turn a deep rusty color and dead fish would float by our swimming hole. We had no idea what was causing the rusty-colored water but we knew it was not safe. This began my interest in environmental concerns in my adult life.

Having a swimming hole was almost a tradition among farm boys during the Great Depression. Most did not have indoor plumbing, much less hot water for bathing. So, it was natural to seek out a place to swim. Two purposes were served: we had a lot of fun and we washed-off yesterdays sweat. Towels or soap were not necessary at our swimming hole. We let Mother Nature take care of drying our hair. We happily put our clothes back on and made our walk back home by way of the railroad track. We were dry by the time we got home.

Isaac Walton League

The early 1960s were times of greater environmental awareness throughout the country. Rachel Carson had just published "Silent Spring," and great interest had developed in the writings of Aldo Leopold. This was also a time when many new conservation organizations developed, and others experienced increased interest and membership.

I became a member of the Isaac Walton League due to my life-long interests in nature and nature related activities. About two years later I was elected president of the Springfield chapter. Being in this organization caused me to think about some of the environmental problems that I had witnessed throughout my life.

I had vivid memories of the times when the water of the South Fork River would be a deep rust color. This usually happened after especially large amounts of rain had fallen. As a child, I did not know the cause of the change in watercolor, but I would soon learn that it was associated with the coal mine located near Kincaid.

In those days it was common for the coal companies to pile the waste or "gob" in piles on the land surface next to the mine. There have been 58 operating coalmines in Sangamon County, and most of these mines had a refuse pile, or "gob pile".

When rainwater passed through the gob pile, acid, iron, and other compounds were dissolved, and that turned the water a deep rust color. Most of this water drained into the South Fork. Sometimes the quantity was so great that it turned the river water a rusty color. This rusty color lasted for days before it was finally washed downstream.

This drainage was very harmful to the fish. As a child I remember how the dead fish would float downstream and get caught in logjams or stranded on the banks. The fishing always changed following one of these rusty water episodes. Even though the water had cleared, no one would be able to catch any fish for several days or weeks. It was apparent that most or all of the fish had been killed.

We never did swim in the river during the times that the water was colored by the acid drainage. If it was harmful to the fish, it seemed likely that it could also be harmful to people. We didn't know for sure, but we also didn't want to find out.

I eventually determined that the cause of the "rusty water" was the drainage off of the gob or waste pile at the coalmine near Kincaid. It was a problem that I thought needed to be addressed.

We began to contact Peabody Coal Company to inform them of our concern regarding the South Fork River. They were receptive to our concerns, and stated that they would cooperate in efforts to prevent future acid mine drainage from entering the South Fork.

We held meetings in Springfield and at the mine site near Kincaid where we could see the gob piles that were the cause of the problem. The idea of covering these piles with several feet of dirt soon developed, and everyone thought that this would be a good solution to the problem. Grass would be sown on the dirt to establish some vegetation once the work of covering the piles had been completed.

Peabody Coal took this idea and applied it to all of their gob piles throughout Illinois. Every one of them was covered within a few years.

Peabody developed some advertisements to let people know that they had completed this work. Perhaps they were hoping that these efforts would help improve their environmental image with the public.

It wasn't long before some state and federal laws were developed that regulated acid mine drainage. Our efforts locally with Peabody helped begin the process.

It has now been many years since the waters of the South Fork were a rusty red color. There haven't been any fish kills, and the quality of the river water seems to be greatly improved over what it was like forty years ago.

Another project that we completed while I was president was the development of the Abraham Lincoln Canoe Trail on the Sangamon River. This trail began at the Lincoln Homestead site near Decatur and ended at Lincoln's New Salem Historic Site near Petersburg.

This was the first home in Illinois for Lincoln's parents. Young Abe rafted down the Sangamon from this site, and his raft got caught on a temporary dam at New Salem in Menard County. Some of the men helped him get the raft off of the dam, and Lincoln became acquainted with them. That was the beginning of his residence in the village of New Salem. This was also the reason why we selected this stretch of the river for the canoe trail.

A ceremony that included Governor Otto Kerner was held at the Lincoln Homestead Park where a sign was placed that indicated the beginning of the trail. Approximately 100 people attended the meeting, and our son George played taps on his trumpet at the close of the ceremony. Then fifteen canoes, each containing four people, left on the inaugural canoe trip down the Sangamon.

We had to portage around the big logjam near Roby, and we canoed through the rapids not far from this logjam. I was canoeing with my three boys and we were able to get through these areas without much trouble.

There were many sights to see as we passed down the stream. There were large trees with their root systems exposed, large rocks in the water, rock cliffs, cabins, an iron bridge, and numerous other things along the river that people had made.

I got out of the canoe at Carpenter Park at Springfield and the boys continued on. They didn't have any big problems, except that Jim lost his glasses when they were getting out of the canoe at New Salem. The boys looked for them and managed to find them in about four feet of water within a few minutes. We were pretty lucky.

The canoe trail was a great experience for all of us. The trail was a joint venture with the Department of Conservation, and many people have used it through the years. This stretch of the Sangamon is a popular canoe route to this day.

Home Life

Toby

Around 1952, my family first met Toby in Loami. It seems he was a distant cousin of my wife and had come to Loami looking for a place to live. He was about 50 years old at the time and had never really held any type of steady work. He worked for a while at a shoe factory in Chester, Illinois, but became upset when his employer wanted to take social security from his paycheck. That was Toby's last day working at the shoe factory.

Apparently, Toby had been going from one relative to another where he stayed for a while, but soon stayed beyond his welcome. That's how he ended up in Loami, hoping to find another relative who would give him a place to live. Toby hoped he could find a farm, because he knew farm work and wanted to live in the country.

When Toby learned we had a farm, he wanted to live with us and help with the chores. He didn't want any pay, just food to eat and a roof overhead. It didn't seem like much, but that's all that he wanted. It wasn't long before Toby was living with my family on the farm in Rochester.

We soon learned Toby had not gone far in school. He quit about the fifth grade and never returned. We suspected that Toby never really had much of a home life; he mentioned once that his parents had separated. If we were sure of anything, we knew their family was very poor.

Toby never learned to drive a car or a tractor, and that limited his use around the farm. He could mow the yard, though, and he helped my wife with the chores around the house. He pumped water for the livestock and usually helped with the hay harvest. Toby knew how to take care of the livestock and was careful to avoid our ram, Oscar, when he was in the barnyard.

Toby loved to keep our lawn looking good

One of Toby's favorite activities was hunting. He liked the outdoors and had loved to go hunting with his buddies in Randolph County. I bought Toby a 12-gauge shotgun and a bird dog, and he hunted on the farm during the hunting seasons. He had several hunting dogs through the years, but his last dog, Annie, was one of his favorites. She was a blue-tick hound. Although hounds are used mostly for coon hunting, Toby didn't care. He took Annie to hunt rabbits and quail.

Toby was very fond of our children and there was little he wouldn't do for them. He helped the children read when they were small, but when he didn't understand certain words, he would skip the page. As our children grew older, they would catch him skipping pages. After awhile, the children were reading to Toby.

When the children were big enough to attend school, Toby always made sure the kids got home safely, especially during cold, winter weather. There were times when he would walk to school and meet one of our kids. Sometimes he actually carried them home if there was snow or ice on the ground.

Toby was always around the house, and we didn't have to worry about the children. When a stranger came around, Toby asked them what they wanted, and he often told them they needed to be going. He was always keeping track of the people who came by the farm.

Toby had some habits that contributed to his declining health. He smoked Camel cigarettes and would smoke an entire carton in a day if he had them. We had to ration his cigarettes and his whiskey. I took him to the stockyards in Springfield once and gave him a few dollars to go to the tavern for a drink. When I went to retrieve him, I found him singing away in the tavern.

When Toby was about 70 years old, he developed congestive heart failure. He was admitted to the hospital in Springfield where he stayed for a few days, but soon returned to our home. We cared for Toby at home for a few months, but passed away one night. We were all very saddened. We buried him with his family in a small cemetery in the hills of Randolph County where he wanted to be buried.

On his Headstone, I had Toby's name and the dates of his birth and death engraved. Above the dates was a depiction of a man hunting quail with a dog. I also had an inscription placed on the lower side of the back of the stone that gives the names of our five children. These were the things in life dearest to him. Our children have fond memories of Toby to this day.

Bartering Chickens for Rugs

In the fall of 1935, a big black car pulled into the driveway of our home. They had dark complexions, much like the gypsies that came to the cabin for wood, so we assumed that they were also gypsies. There were two men and two women. They came to the door and said that they had fine oriental rugs for sale. My mother had always wanted some oriental rugs, so they had her attention.

After listening to their sales pitch for a while, one of the men said these rugs are fireproof. He jumped up and proceeded to light a newspaper on fire. He then held the fire to the bottom of one of the rugs. My dad yelled at him and told him to "Put that fire out. You're going to burn the house down". The fire was soon out, and dad was happy.

After talking for several minutes, an agreement was made that 75 young chickens would be traded for two 12 x 12 rugs. Our mother told my brother and me to go out to the chicken yard and catch 75 chickens and tie them together with baling twine. We caught the chickens and tied their feet together so that we had about ten in each group. We helped the gypsies load the chickens into their car.

About 15 minutes passed, and there was a knock at the door. It was the gypsies, and they were saying that six chickens had gotten loose while they were driving, and had returned to our barnyard. My brother and I had to go out to get six more chickens to give to the gypsies.

We were doubtful of their story, but our dad said it was easier to give them more chickens than to try to deal with them. The rugs did last for many years, and our mother was glad to have them. The gypsies never did return to try to sell us more rugs.

The Airplane

I was just a small boy when my older cousin, Bernard Taft, decided he wanted to be an airplane mechanic. It was 1928 and aviation was not nearly as advanced as it is today. There were very few airports, and the thought of commercial flights was yet to develop.

Central Illinois, especially Rochester, was not the place for anyone to study airplane mechanics. After some deliberation, Bernard decided that Kansas City was the place to go. He packed his suitcases and headed west.

While he was in school, he became friends with another student named Carl who was studying to become a pilot. They instantly became good friends and shared their hopes and dreams with each other. One dream they shared was to own an airplane.

It seemed like the perfect combination to "Barnstorm" around the country. Carl was going to be a pilot and Bernard was going to be an airplane mechanic. One would fly the plane and the other would keep it in good running condition. The latter was especially important because the engines during that time had the nasty habit of quitting from time to time.

Speaking of being reliable, the engine was the only thing on the aircraft that was metal. The plane was a wooden frame covered with cloth that had been painted so the air could not pass through it. Even the propeller was made of wood.

My grandfather loaned Bernard some money, and together they bought an early Waco biplane. They flew it from Kansas City back to Rochester. You might think Carl and Bernard landed at the airport in Springfield when they got to Illinois, but they didn't. They landed in the pasture just east of the cemetery on our farm in Rochester. Our pasture became their runway when the cows weren't in the way. My dad was in the barn milking cows when the plane arrived. It was probably the first airplane to land in Rochester, and the sound of the engine startled the cows. The cow my dad was milking was so startled; she kicked over the bucket of milk.

Bernard with his Waco Biplane

My parents told me that Carl and Bernard thought they could make a lot of money barnstorming the area and taking people for rides. Practically every little town had some type of picnic or fair in those days, and the young men planned to take their biplane to as many of these events as possible.

Speaking of cows, they were naturally curious about this new object that had appeared in their pasture, and went to investigate. There must have been something about the cloth on the plane that the cows liked, because they began to lick the plane in several places. This licking continued for days, and when Carl and Bernard went to fly their plane, they found several holes in it. They had to order some cloth, glue and paint to repair the holes.

After the repair work was finished, they were ready to fly to Williamsville for their local fair. Bernard could not go for some reason, so Carl got one of our neighbors, Calvin Eggleston, to go with him. Carl was flying the plane, and with Calvin, they made the trip to Williamsville. Calvin's mother had warned him to stay away from those Taft boys and that crazy flying contraption, but Calvin had climbed into the plane without his mother's knowledge.

The flight to Williamsville was made without any trouble, but the plane wasn't running properly on the trip back to the cow pasture at Rochester. No matter how hard he tried, Carl could not get the plane to gain altitude. They were traveling just above the level of the trees and were probably thinking they were going to have to make an emergency landing at some suitable place. Their best hope was to make it back to our cow pasture.

They were getting along fine until they came to Dawson. There was an electrical transmission line there and Carl must not have seen it. The plane hit the line, crashed to the ground and was completely destroyed except for the propeller. Carl and Calvin were both injured, but their injuries were not life threatening. They were both lucky to be alive. Carl had more injuries than Calvin. He was confined to bed for almost a month in my grandfathers home before he was able to travel.

Carl left and we never heard any more from him for well over thirty years, until one day in the summer of 1958, there was a knock at the door. I answered the knock and learned that the visitor was Carl, who was back in Rochester visiting friends. Carl had been living in California where he owned a shoe store. He was back in Illinois on vacation with his family.

It was great to see him after so many years and our conversation eventually drifted to that fateful day and the airplane. I told Carl that I had the propeller and asked him if he would like to see it. We looked at that propeller and I took out my pocketknife and cut a sliver of wood for him to take home. Then I showed him a photograph of Bernard standing next to the plane in the pasture.

Had Bernard been with Carl on that fateful day so many years ago, perhaps he could have fixed the engine problem. The plane was destroyed, but no one lost their life in the crash. Who knows what future in aviation Carl and Bernard might have had if the plane had not crashed. Bernard did not pursue a career in aviation mechanics. Instead, he spent his life as an automobile mechanic. Carl never flew another airplane, and eventually became a shoe salesman. Their dream of flying did not last beyond the summer of 1928.

The Young's

There was a family in Rochester named Young, and its family members were friends of my dad. I became acquainted with the boys who I went to school with during my school years. The father was the custodian at the Rochester School, and he later got a job at Sangamo Electric in Springfield. He bought a lot on Dirksen Drive in Springfield, which was known as the bypass at that time. Around 1940, Mr. Young started to build a home on the land he had bought. Mr. Young went to Missouri and got some sandstone slabs that were used on the sides of the house. There were no other houses in the vicinity at that time and no trees. The area had been farmed until just before he bought the land.

After building the house, Mr. Young decided he needed some trees. He came down to our farm and went to the river where he selected two sycamore saplings about ten feet tall. We dug these trees up and put them in a box wagon hitched to a team of horses. I hauled them into town for him and we planted the trees in his front yard. As of this date, these trees are still thriving and are about three feet in diameter. They can be seen if you drive by the old Young home place on Dirksen. As the trees matured, so too did the neighborhood. The house still has the sandstone slabs that were hauled to Springfield from Missouri.

Two of the older Young boys, Carl and Walter, were friends of mine. Both of them were in World War II. Carl was in the Army and Walter in the Marine Corps. There was a younger brother named Don who was also a friend of mine. Don had just bought a new bicycle and was in uptown Rochester one night about 10:00 P.M. One of the men sitting on the "Liars Bench" asked him how long it would take to ride home. Don told the man he could ride home in less than an hour, but the man did not believe he could. Don bet 25 cents that he would be home in less than an hour. He made it home in 46 minutes and quickly phoned the man to let him know. The man said: "I owe you a quarter". Don agreed and rode back out to Rochester to pick up his quarter.

Don was about 15 years old when he started helping me on the farm. He lost his wallet one spring while he was disking and could not find it anywhere. The following spring, I was plowing when I saw this billfold lying in the furrow in front of the tractor. I stopped to pick it up and found it was Don's. It was intact, and it even had a one-dollar bill and a few pictures of two of his best girlfriends. Don was in disbelief when I returned it to him.

Don became a policeman and detective in Springfield, and he eventually was known as one of the best detectives in the area. He now runs a private detective agency, and one of his sons has followed in the footsteps and works for the Springfield Police Department.

Trip to the Holy Land

In the early spring of 1970, we received a flyer from Lincoln Christian College in Lincoln, Illinois advertising a trip to the Holy Land. It was a 52-day trip that included stops in 20 countries for what seemed a bargain price of $1,600, all expenses paid, for each person.

My wife and I decided we would go. The price was good, and we had never been to the Holy Land. The timing also seemed good because there was stability in the region at the time. I believed we should visit the area before trouble developed, and the region literally" blew up."

Our trip started in St. Louis, so a friend drove us to Lambert Field where we boarded a plane bound for New York. All members of our travel group assembled in New York City to organize before our initial flight to Shannon, Ireland.

Our flight to Shannon took six hours. We boarded a bus upon our arrival and traveled through the southern part of Ireland to County Cork, the location of Blarney Castle and the famous Blarney stone. Many consider this county to be where St. Patrick lived. According to legend, St. Patrick drove all the snakes out of Ireland.

It was a short trip to our next stop in Glasgow, Scotland. From Glasgow we traveled to Edinburgh where we stopped for lunch at a small restaurant. I noticed Haggis on the menu and decided to try some. It didn't turn out to be a very pleasurable experience, and I decided I really didn't want to eat Haggis again. Fortunately, the visit to Sterling Castle more than made up for the Haggis. The castle has a rich history linked to William Wallace and Robert the Bruce, two early leaders who fought for Scotland's freedom. We also had a chance to visit the grave of John Knox, founder of the Presbyterian Church.

Our next stop was London where we visited Windsor Castle, Oxford University, Westminster Abbey, St. Paul's Cathedral and Hampton Court, the home of the Stewart royal family. We traveled north of London to Nottingham Woods, the legendary home of Robin Hood and his merry band. There was a monastery not far from the woods where the High Sheriff used to distribute food to people more than a thousand years ago.

After Great Britain, we traveled to Paris. We visited the Eiffel Tower, Versailles Palace, and Notre Dame Cathedral, the site where the famous movie, The Hunchback, was filmed. Our three days in Paris were very enjoyable, but we were soon preparing to leave for the Netherlands.

Amsterdam was fascinating. This was the first time that we had seen the canals and windmills that we had heard of for so many years.

While we were traveling, I became very interested in the espalier pruning used on their fruit trees. I have since wanted to prune my apple trees like theirs.

The next part of our tour was a bus ride to Cologne, Germany where we saw the Cologne Cathedral on the Rhine River. We were also impressed with Bavaria in the southern part of Germany where we visited Oberammergau, the site of the Passion Play. According to legend, the Black Death spared this town during the 1400's, so they conduct this play as their way of giving thanks. Everyone involved in the Passion Play must be born in Oberammergau. We were fortunate to see the play, but it was longer than any play we had ever seen in America. It started at 8:00 in the morning and finished at 4:00 in the afternoon.

After Oberammergau, we traveled through Austria and Switzerland to Milan, Italy. There were many paintings and artifacts associated with Leonardo Da Vinci in Milan. We saw the leaning tower of Pisa and the spectacular Tivoli Gardens, near Rome, where there are many fountains, possibly 1,000 or more, that are lighted at night.

While in Rome, we were nearly out of clean clothing, so I went out to find a Laundromat. I was having trouble with the language, so I asked a policeman if he knew the location of a Laundromat. He directed me to a girl who did laundry for people. She did our laundry, and I returned to our hotel in a reasonable time.

While in Rome, we saw a portion of the old Roman highway, the Apian Way. We also visited the Coliseum and the Vatican where we saw Da Vinci's paintings on the ceiling of the Sistine Chapel. It was also arranged for us to have an audience with the Pope.

Greece was our next destination. It was a very pretty country with groves of orange and olive trees. We traveled to Corinth, the site of one of the earliest churches, and the church that Paul wrote to in his

Letters to the Corinthians. Next, we went to Athens, where we visited the Acropolis, the site of the Parthenon and many ancient artifacts.

Our next stop was the site of the early church at Ephesus in Turkey. Paul's Letters to the Ephesians were written to this church. In addition, the apostle John is buried in Ephesus.

We went to Istanbul for two days, and while there, we visited the Grand Bazaar, or the largest flea market in the world. We also went to a Sultan's palace where we saw a dog's bed said to be worth five million dollars. This bed was made in China, and is decorated with many jewels. Istanbul is also where Hagia Sophia, a Byzantine cathedral, and the Blue Mosque are located. Before we could enter either building, we had to remove our shoes.

We flew from Istanbul to Beirut, Lebanon. This was before the city was destroyed by the civil war. It was a beautiful city with wonderful hotels and modern conveniences. While in Beirut, we saw an 80-foot statue of the Virgin Mary. We traveled from Beirut to Baalback, a city built to honor Baal. It was a thriving city in a fertile valley about 2,000 years ago, but several earthquakes have since destroyed much of this city.

From Lebanon, we flew to Cairo, Egypt where we rode camels to see the pyramids at Giza. We saw many other fascinating sights, including the Nile River, the old Christian sector and the Cairo Bazaar. From Cairo, we went to Tel Aviv, Israel. During this time, we could not go directly to Israel from Egypt because of political tensions. We had to fly to Cyprus first, and then board an airliner for the flight to the Holy Land. The greatest number of days would be spent there.

We boarded a bus after landing in Tel Aviv that took us to our hotel in the walled city of Old Jerusalem. This hotel would serve as our base-of-operations for the next two weeks. A trip to a well-known Biblical site departed from this hotel each day. The first trip was to the Mount of Olives where we had a good view of the Temple Mount and the gold-domed mosque in the City of Old Jerusalem. Our next trip was to a church on the Mount of Olives named after Mary and Martha, the sisters of Lazarus. This same trip included a visit to the tomb of Lazarus. This tomb appeared to be a natural cave in solid rock, but it had been modified to serve as a tomb.

One of the unique experiences of the trip was an opportunity to go swimming in the Sea of Galilee. We went to Tiberius, an old Roman outpost, and got into the sea there. I found walking along the sea difficult due to the sharp cobblestones. Once we had finished our swim, we took a boat across the Sea to Capernaum, the home of Peter.

Another special trip was to Nazareth where Christ was raised. We saw Mary's home, Joseph's carpenter shop, and one of the most beautiful churches that I have ever seen. It is built like an inverted lily flower and contained beautiful stained glass. It is known as the Church of the Enunciation.

One of the memorable visits while we were in Bethlehem was to the Church of the Nativity. It was most impressive! It is a huge church, and it is considered to be the site where Christ was born.

Our trip to Jericho gave us a sense of the importance of this place in Biblical history. We saw the excavations on the walls and learned much about the history of the site.

One of our last trips was to the caves near Qumran, where the Dead Sea Scrolls were found. These are natural caves where people lived for many years. These scrolls were prepared by a group of monks and kept in the caves. The climate ensured their long survival.

While staying in Jerusalem, I became acquainted with a young boy named Jimmy. He was a Palestinian who lived in Jerusalem. Jimmy shined my shoes every morning, and we soon became friends. He would come to the hotel in the afternoon and we would hike to Old Jerusalem to look at many different sights. I saw many things that were not on our normal tour list because of Jimmy.

One morning he took me to Hezekiah's tunnel. This tunnel was made through the mountains about 800 BC, to carry water to the city from the spring of Gihon in the Kidron Valley, to the Pool of Siloam in the old City of David. There was great fear that the Babylonians would lay siege to the city, and they would not be able to get water. Work on the tunnel began on opposite sides of the mountain and joined together in the middle with near perfect alignment. Not bad engineering for that era. When we arrived at the tunnel, I took off my shoes and waded in with Jimmy. It was completely dark, and I did not have anything to protect my feet. The water was cold, and ranged from knee deep to waist deep. The tunnel is more than 2000 feet long. There have been many people visit the Holy Land, but not many of them have waded through Hezekiah's tunnel. Many thanks to Jimmy.

This was a wonderful trip for both of us, and we learned many wonderful things about these 20 countries. This trip also gave Mardell and I a better understanding of how Christianity got started and eventually came to America 2,000 years after its beginning in the Holy Land.

Life on the Farm

Hay Baling

I was home from the university and there was a need for someone to help bale hay. It was wartime, so I could not buy a new hay baler. My neighbor Gene Young said I could use his for 3 cents a bale. I worked all summer baling alfalfa, red clover, timothy, and straw, and any other type of hay that needed to be baled.

I was using a Case baler that required one person to feed the wires around the bales and another to tie them. The tractor I used was a 1936 WC Allis Chalmers. Unlike modern tractors, it did not have a starter, so I had to crank it to start it. I used to run the tractor and two boys operated the wire tying on the baler.

There were times when the tractor would not start because the magneto ignition would short out. I had to take it off and take it into town for repairs. I had trouble with the timing after the repairs were made, but I eventually learned how to reset the magneto to the same position it was in when it was removed.

The Case baler had a V4, air-cooled Wisconsin engine, and it gave us more trouble than starting the tractor. It also had to be cranked, just like the tractor. When we had trouble getting the baler engine to start, there was a guy who would hold on to a spark plug wire to see if there was any spark coming from the magneto.

I baled hay all over the county. I was four miles north of Dawson where I baled 120 acres of red clover hay for a guy named Jim Cravens. He made a deal with me in which I got half of the hay. I was to put his half in his the barn. I managed to sell my half for a dollar a bale, and the buyer came to the field, picked up the bales, and loaded them on his truck.

We baled a lot of timothy hay at Buckhart in the 1940s, and it was awfully dirty work. We would run the baler until it used a roll of wire, and then we would swim in the gravel pits for a while before reloading the baler with wire and starting again.

I also went east to Roby, and south as far as New City. There were a number of small hay fields around Lake Springfield that I baled. None of the fields were larger than 20 acres, but there was close to 400 acres total.

The author in his new 1946 Ford truck

I bought a truck in 1946 and began to haul hay and put it into barns for 25 cents a bale. My truck was a 1946 Ford F6 that had a flathead V8 engine, a two-speed axle, and a 14 foot bed. If we stacked the hay just right, we could get 108 bales on this truck. We had to tie the bales down if we had to travel on the road for any length of time.

We had a great time baling almost every day. The crew always had something funny going on. For drinks, Norman Braner had the idea of buying a large selection of soda and mixing them all together in the drinking cooler. It had a drinking spout on it and we would all share the refreshment. It tasted a little different each day.

One day, we had a near disaster. We were transporting all of our equipment to a new hay field close to Hill Top. We had to go down route 29 with me driving the tractor, which had the baler in tow behind. One of the guys wanted to ride with me on the tractor, so he sat on the fender. Some other crewmember was driving the new truck. Since we were on the highway, I had the WC in road gear and our speed was about 15 mph. There was some Tom Foolery going on between the boy on the fender and the crew in the truck. They managed to run the truck into the tractor and threw my passenger off in front of the tractor tire. He was run over first by the tractor, followed shortly there after by the hay baler tire. Fortunately, there was not much traffic on the highway. We pulled off, onto the side of the road as quick as possible, and went to see about him. He seemed very lifeless, but shortly he rolled his eyes, looked at us and said, "What happened". He had two tire tracks imprinted across his chest. Pretty soon, he got up and a neighbor passing by took him to the hospital. Thankfully, all that was wrong was a broken wrist.

In 1948, I bought a new automatic, self-tying, twine baler from a dealer in Pawnee. Norman Braner and I went to the dealership to pick it up. We had the truck with the tractor loaded on the bed to pull the baler back home. We were unloading the tractor at the railroad unloading dock, and Norman was driving the tractor off of the truck. The truck wasn't in gear properly, and it began to move forward. Norman kept driving the tractor off of the truck, but the back wheels did not get to the loading dock before the truck rolled away. The tractor fell off of the dock, and was hanging by the front wheels. Norman was not hurt, and he was still sitting on the tractor with the engine running. The seat was bent some, but nothing else was damaged. We managed to back the tractor off of the dock, and Norman pulled the new baler home.

I used the new baler for about four years. I did not do any more custom baling after 1952. I kept the baler, but it sat outside for years. A guy came by one day and offered to take all of my old implements away. One of those implements was the old hay baler.

Oscar the Hardhead

One of the facts of early farm life for us kids was that we had to find our own entertainment. Sometimes we would go swimming, or we would play on top of a straw stack left from threshing. We would play for hours on the straw until darkness came or there were chores to be completed. Most of our fun was baseball or swimming, but there were a few years when we had a rather unusual form of entertainment.

We always raised a few sheep during the early days on my father's farm. We had one buck during the 1940s that we called Oscar. Oscar was a big, strong ram that my dad obtained, hoping that he would father extra fine lambs. Raising sheep was a common practice in those days, and many of the local farms had a flock of sheep. Oscar was a purebred Shopshire with an impressive family bloodline.

Oscar wasn't your typical mild-mannered sheep. He was very aggressive, and would ram into any person that turned their back on him. He could never be trusted, and we were always careful to watch him whenever we were close to him. If he sensed an opportunity, he would ram into any person that came into the barnyard. Even other animals weren't safe, regardless of their size. We learned this one-day when he managed to knock our bull down.

My brother and I had noticed how Oscar would charge at practically anything, so we got the idea of using the old wheelbarrow as a battering ram against him. One of us rode in the wheelbarrow while the other pushed it as fast as he could toward Oscar. Oscar would see us coming and take off running toward the wheelbarrow as fast as he could go. He would smack into the wheelbarrow and bounce off. The person in the wheelbarrow would usually land on Oscar or fly through the air over him. We would get up, trade places and run at him again.

There were plenty of weekend afternoons when we spent hours ramming into Oscar with that wheelbarrow. Our entertainment with Oscar became a community event, and the neighbor boys would come over to watch and join in on the fun. We would go after Oscar until we got tired, but Oscar never seemed to get tired. There were days when a large crowd gathered to watch the fun that lasted most of the afternoon. He never stopped charging at the wheelbarrow, and we never did manage to knock him out. There were times when we would hit Oscar so hard that the rider would fly out and land in the barnyard behind Oscar. Everyone figured that he had a pretty hard head.

Our fun with Oscar continued for three years, but it ended rather abruptly one day when our mother came into the barnyard. She forgot about the aggressiveness of Oscar and turned her back on him. Oscar had been watching, and he hit her from the back and sent her flying into the mud. He hurt her ribs and got her pretty muddy. Most of all, she was pretty angry with Oscar, and a little bit perturbed with us. She told us that we were responsible for what had happened because we kept ramming Oscar with the wheelbarrow. It wasn't long after this incident that he was gone from the farm. In his three years with us, Oscar became a local legend.

Many years have passed since we pushed our wheelbarrow at Oscar, but memories of him remain to this day. Oscar did leave more than just memories. He fathered many very nice lambs while he on the farm. Fortunately, as far as I know, none of his offspring took the challenge of charging into a steel wheelbarrow, pushed by young boys.

Oscar on a good day

Buying Angus Cattle

I was about twenty years old when my dad and I went to a farm near Scottville, in Macoupin County. It was owned by Benny Ellis and his sister Lucibra. It was a cold day in late November during the early 1940s. My dad was hoping that he could buy 25 to 30 Angus calves. We took our truck in order to haul them back to our farm in Rochester.

Mr. Ellis greeted us when we arrived. He was dressed conservatively in bib overalls, a coat, a felt hat, and gloves. Based upon what he told us, his parents had owned the farm and he had spent his entire life there, as had his sister. They had a car in the garage, and it seemed to have something wrong with it because it was sitting on concrete blocks. When we inquired, he told us that he had jacked the car up and put it away for the winter.

It took us a while to select and load the cattle onto our truck, but we managed to finish just before lunch. Mr. Ellis asked if we would like to join him and his sister for lunch. We said that it was very kind of him to ask us into his home. As we sat down for lunch meal, I noticed that his sister had fried about 20 eggs and that she was serving them along with ground-wheat that she had made into a type of porridge. There was little doubt that everything served had been produced on their farm. It was very filling and I can't remember having a lunch like that before or since.

We made one more trip to the Ellis farm the next year to buy more cattle. We stayed for lunch again, and were served the same fried eggs and ground-wheat porridge. It might have been what they had for lunch every day.

I lost track of the Ellis's through the years, but I do know that Benny passed away many years ago. His sister lived much longer and has since passed away about 10 years ago. Her last request was to burn the old Ellis home when she died.

They lived their entire lives on the farm established by their parents. Their way of life was different, but it is also likely that their way of living was shaped by the Great Depression. Many people of their age lived in fear that it would return again, so they lived their lives with that thought in mind. Clothes, cars, tools, and other items were used until they "Got the good out of them." They did not discard anything until this was done.

Home Butchering

It was common for most of the farms to be almost self-sufficient. We raised our own fruits, vegetables, chickens, eggs, and milk. We also produced our own beef, pork, and lamb. Of these, pork was the one meat that we produced in the greatest quantities.

Like other jobs on the farm, such as threshing, the neighbors all helped with the butchering. Butchering took place at one farm on one weekend, and another one on the following weekend. All of our butchering was done outside during the fall or early winter months.

We kept three big cast iron kettles on the farm just for butchering. These kettles fit into a large metal ring, having three legs that kept the kettle from resting on the ground. When the butchering day arrived, we started a fire under these kettles and kept it burning throughout the day. We always made sure that we had plenty of wood so the fires did not go out.

There were several reasons for butchering in the fall. The cooler weather made the work much more comfortable, especially around the hot fires. It also helped keep the meat from spoiling. Another reason for butchering in the fall was that this was the time when apples and pears were ripe. They were mixed with the pork and spices to make mincemeat.

Mincemeat was prepared by cooking ground, lean pork with apples, cinnamon, alum, and allspice. My grandfather often made 15 to 20 gallons of mincemeat in one of the big black, cast iron kettles. Its preparation kept at least one person busy stirring the mixture for two or three hours until it was completely cooked.

We usually butchered four hogs that weighed about two hundred pounds each. Hogs that were larger than this were too difficult to handle. The butchering began when the hogs were shot and killed.

A shot into the front part of the head was preferred to a shot into the heart or some other vital organ. Their throat was then cut so the blood would drain from them.

Not all of the shots were successful in killing the hogs. Sometimes the individuals doing the butchering did a little drinking, and their aim wasn't so accurate. The hogs would be stunned, but they would get up and run away.

We then cut the skin on the lower part of the back legs of the hogs to reveal the large tendon that we used to hang them. We called the cutting of the skin to reveal this tendon, gambling. We ran a strong pole through the underneath side of this tendon and used it for handling the hogs. Some people used a block and tackle to lift the hogs, but ours were usually light enough to be easily handled by a few men.

All of the hogs had to be scalded by dipping them into a barrel full of boiling hot water that contained some Lewis Lye. The object was to get the hairs off of the hogs skin, and the hot water and Lewis Lye helped start this process. Once the hogs were scalded, they were scraped with a round-shaped scraper to remove the hair.

We had to be careful around the Lewis Lye. It was very caustic, and skin could be burned or eyes damaged if it splashed on them. For this reason, none of the children were allowed to come close to the barrel or kettle where the scalding was taking place.

All of their entrails were removed, like the heart, liver, kidneys, and intestines. We ate the heart and liver, and some people cleaned the intestines and stuffed them with sausage. Our mother never used the intestines. Some people would split the skull, remove the brain, and fry it. They said that they used everything from the hog but the squeal.

There were parts of the hog that could be made into toys. I remember butchering as a small boy, when an older man was removing the entrails from a hog. He told me to go get a large turkey feather for him. He took this feather, took out his pocketknife, and removed the large quill end. After cutting off the other end of the quill, he stuck the quill into the opening of the urinary bladder that he had just removed. He stuck the other end of the quill into his mouth and blew air into the bladder until it was about the size of a soccer ball. Then he tied the urinary duct closed with a piece of string, and removed the feather. This bladder became leathery with time, and we played with it for several years. He was the only person that I ever knew that made a toy out of the urinary bladder of a pig.

Once the hog was ready, the sides were removed to make bacon. The large upper legs were removed to make hams. Any extra lean meat was added to what would become sausage. My job was to cut up any fat and toss it into the cast iron kettle that was being used to make lard. This fat would cook, and much of the fat would come out. The cooked fatty meat was taken out and put into a lard press, which removed the remaining lard. The cooked meat that was left over from the cooking and pressing was called "cracklins." We nibbled on the cracklins, but most of them were thrown over into the chicken yard for the chickens to eat.

The hot fat or lard was dipped out of the kettles and poured into large cans or "lard buckets." The lard was allowed to cool and lids were put on them until they were needed for cooking. Most everyone in those days did all of their frying using lard. Lard was also used to make piecrusts.

The lean meat that we cut up was ground and ready to make into sausage. Generally, there was a person who was the expert at mixing the spices for the sausage. The spices always included sage, pepper, salt, and sometimes mustard seed. Because our mother didn't like using the cleaned intestines, we always stuffed our sausage in a white cloth known as muslin. This cloth had to be sewed to form a long tube that would hold the sausage. Once the "expert" had added all of the spices to the ground meat, the meat was placed into a sausage press and it was used to fill the muslin tubes made by our mother.

The lower legs of the hogs were also removed and used to make pickled pigs feet. The toes were cut off, and they were cooked in vinegar, water, and spices until they were completely cooked. Then our mother would can them for eating at some later date.

Once all of the hams, bacon, and sausage had been prepared, it was taken to the smoke house. Salt was spread over the hams and bacon, and they were suspended from the ceiling, along with the sausage, to be smoked. There were no refrigerators, so salt and smoking were important ways of curing and preserving meat for the warmer months. It also gave the meat a very nice flavor.

The smoking process began with the selection of some green, small-sized hickory wood. A fire was started in the center of the floor of the smokehouse, usually in a ring or circle of stones, and the green hickory was added to the fire. The green hickory wood would produce a dense smoke that would flavor and preserve the meat. The smoking would continue for days until the desired effect had been reached.

We ate bacon, ham, and sausage throughout the winter months, but the approach of warm weather meant that we had to "cook down" the sausage. All of the remaining sausage was carried into the kitchen, sliced, and cooked. After it had cooled, it was placed in the bottom of a large stone jar. We put as much cooked sausage into the jar as we could. Then melted lard was poured into the jar so that all of the sausage was completely covered. This method would preserve the sausage for use during the summer. I remember going to these jars and reaching down through the lard to get sausage for my mother.

We saved the grease from cooking bacon and sausage and used it to make soap. This soap was made with Lewis Lye, and was called lye soap by many people. It wasn't a gentle soap, but it was often the only soap that many people had for their bathing and cleaning.

Home butchering is an event of the past now. Government regulations, refrigeration, and changes in our society have made it disappear. It is regretful in many ways because it was one of the events of the earlier years that brought families and friends together. It was hard work, but it brought great rewards.

Making Apple Butter

Apple butter making was always done in the fall when the apples had reached their peak ripeness. We would go to an orchard and pick up as many as ten burlap bags of apples. My wife and my mother plus several other women would spend several days peeling and cutting up the apples. This work was made easier by using a peeler. They did not have to be perfect and free of blemishes, but all of the rotten areas or insect damage had to be removed.

A 40 gallon copper kettle was used to make the apple butter. A good fire was started and the kettle was placed over the fire. A gallon of pure apple cider was poured into the kettle, and two silver dollars were put in with the cider. The cider was necessary to start the cooking process, and the silver dollars were there to keep the apple butter from sticking to the kettle when cooking.

The cooking would take most of the day, and the butter had to be stirred with a wooden paddle throughout the cooking process. I called the paddle that we used a "horse-head" paddle. The handle was made of bamboo, and the paddle was Oak wood. The paddle was attached at a right angle to the handle, and had holes in it to make the stirring and mixing easier. Constant stirring was necessary as the apple butter was cooking, so we took turns when one person became tired.

Fall was a good time to make apple butter for other reasons. The fire was hot and the cooler temperatures made the work more comfortable and enjoyable. There were fewer insects to contend with during the cool weather, and the heat and smoke helped to keep them away from the apple butter.

Cinnamon, sugar, and other spices were added to the apple butter as it cooked. When it was finished, it was ready to be canned. The quantities of these spices that were added to the butter often depended on what kind of apple being used. My wife and mother canned apple butter in quart-sized Ball jars by placing several jars, filled with apple butter and sealed with a lid, into boiling water for about forty-five minutes. The lids of these jars would seal when they cooled after being taken out of the hot water.

I always liked apple butter making. The smell of cooking apples and the wood smoke were always pleasant. Once we were finished, we had plenty of apple butter for breakfast and other occasions until the next fall. To this day, one of my favorite ways to eat apple butter is on soda biscuits.

Early Farm Life

Illinois is the state where the 4-H programs began the early 1900s. Since its small, humble beginnings, this program has spread to other states, and is now a national organization. It has been of great benefit to thousands of young boys and girls that have an interest in agriculture. This organization promoted education and entertainment for rural youth, and any community of any size had a 4-H organization.

I was about 12 years old when I joined this organization in Rochester. My two brothers and sister also joined 4-H at this time, and we met at different farm homes in the Rochester area. All 4-H activities were sponsored by the University of Illinois Extension service. Our first leader was a man named Wayne Churchill. He was the County Farm Advisor for 4-H in Sangamon County. There was another man named John Churchill, not related to Wayne that was the FFA teacher and another valuable local 4-H leader in Rochester.

The Rochester 4-H Club was one of about 25 in Sangamon County during the 1930s. We interacted with these other clubs, and had judging contests and county livestock judging shows. The winners of these events would compete at shows at the University of Illinois. My cousins, Delbert and Earl Taft, and I won first place in poultry judging at the University in 1936. Our county leader, Wayne Churchill, was proud of our accomplishments, so he took us to the State Journal-Register office and they took our photograph. We were in the paper the next day, along with a story about our accomplishments at the judging contest.

When we entered high school, we became active in FFA, Future Farmers of America. This organization promoted agricultural education, including such things as public speaking, livestock judging and care, and raising of crops. This was a very popular program while I was in high school.

During my high school years, I went to many events where I showed chickens, steers, and sheep. Some of these sheep were the offspring of our ram, Oscar the Hardhead. Our biggest interest was steers, and we took them to many shows and spent considerable time caring and working with them.

While I was a sophomore in high school, I went to a livestock-judging contest at the University of Illinois. I noticed a man working at the cattle barn, so I went to him and told him that I was coming to the university in two years. I wanted to know if he would help me find a job when I arrived. He was the university herdsman, and he had learned his job-tending cattle in his native Scotland. His name was Alex Edgar. He had married a woman from Sangamon County that my mother knew, so I had a way to introduce myself to him. I did get a job working in the cattle barn when I arrived two years later, and it was a big help. I left home with 17 dollars which was enough to pay the first months rent. My job paid 35 cents an hour, and I made enough to pay room and board and didn't need any help from my parents. There were weeks when I worked 40 hours and went to school as well.

Before I left for the university, I won a scholarship from Sears, Roebuck, and Company that paid all of my tuition. My agriculture teacher told me about the potential for getting this scholarship. I had to complete an examination in Springfield at the office of the County Superintendent of Schools, and I was one of two individuals that received a scholarship to the University of Illinois. Sears and Roebuck discontinued this policy of awarding scholarships many years ago.

I learned a lot from Alex Edgar, the Scotch herdsman, on how to handle, care for, and show cattle while I was at the university. One of the most useful things I learned from Alex was how to break a steer to lead. This was a very difficult, but necessary task. We tried everything we could think of to get them to lead, including tying them to a tractor and driving slowly. Nothing worked until he got the idea of tying two steers together by their rope halters. After about a week of being tied together, they would be broke to lead. They did what we couldn't do ourselves. Then they would follow me anywhere. During later years, this knowledge helped me a lot with farming, and I used it every year in caring for cattle, including the Angus cattle that we got from Benny Ellis.

While I was at the university I learned that the best way to be successful in showing steers was to buy one that wasn't quite mature, but showed a lot of potential. He had to have good characteristics of the breed and body conformation to be competitive when entered into shows.

We did very well with our steers. After I came home from the University, I was in 4-H one more year. I had a steer that I raised that was entered in the 4-H Fair and was judged the grand champion. I took this same steer to the Chicago International Livestock Show, which was held in Chicago at the stockyards at 43rd and Halsted Streets. I sold this steer at auction, and then bought some young steers that I thought had lots of potential. I brought these back to Rochester where I cared for them until they were fully developed. We cared for these steers every day, and they became gentle and made great pets.

This young steer had a lot of potential

One day, I was leading one of my champion steers and decided to see if he would climb the steps at the house. He did, so I opened the door and took him inside the house and into the kitchen where my mother was working. Her words were: "Get him out of here." I didn't waste any time turning the steer around and getting him back out the door.

The steers that I bought in Chicago were ready to show in contests the following summer. The steers that we entered, an Angus, a Shorthorn, and a Hereford, won champion for their breed at each fair. We entered these in five county fairs, Sangamon, Macon, Christian, DeWitt, and Logan, and these steers won champion in their breed, and one of the three was always named Grand Champion of the Baby Beef show at each fair. We had similar success with another set of steers the following year.

A "Blue Ribbon" Angus steer

Our success at the fairs for these two years caused some people to become jealous of us. My future wife went to the Logan County Fair with one of her girlfriends, and was watching the steer shows. Her girlfriend remarked: I sure hope someone else wins this show besides

Three Hereford steers I showed at St. Louis

those ***** Taft's. She was disappointed because our steers won all the blue ribbons and the grand champion.

95

After a few years of farming, it was apparent that there was a need for an organization for young adults interested in agriculture, so we organized what was called the Rural Youth in 1947. This consisted of young men and women that had turned 20, and were too old to remain in the 4-H programs. I was elected president of this group in its first year. The county extension office generally referred to it, as a matrimonial society. It did afford opportunities for young farm men and women to meet and socialize.

The Rural Youth proved to be a very valuable organization for a relatively large number of people. I was nominated and selected as the Outstanding Young Farmer of Sangamon County in 1958 by the Springfield Junior Chamber of Commerce, which was quite an honor for me. Although the Rural Youth Organization no longer exists, former members have had some reunions in recent years, and they have been well attended.

The Jeep

At the end of World War II in 1945, there were many Army surplus items, including clothing, tents and vehicles for sale. There were jeeps in Springfield in lines that seemed to be miles long, and many people were buying them for use around the farm or for nostalgic reasons.

A friend of mine came to the farm one day in 1946 with an old Army surplus Jeep. He told me that it was just the thing I needed for use around the farm. It could be used to plow, harrow, pull wagons and perform other farm work. I looked it over and it seemed to run well. It had been painted red and had a cloth top.

The jeep would pull a harrow much faster than a tractor and could be used for many errands, so I bought it. I took the cloth top off and put it in the barn. We used the jeep for a number of jobs around the farm, including feeding cattle and pulling wagons loaded with hay.

I taught our oldest son, George, at an early age how to drive the Jeep. When he was five, George was driving it around the farm. One day when I couldn't drive him to kindergarten, I told him to drive the Jeep. I told him to stay on our farm property and not go on any roads. It wasn't long before he was driving the Jeep to kindergarten every day. Our farmland extended right up to the school property in those days.

George is off to Kindergarten

My wife also used the Jeep to bring water or lunch to me when I was in the field. It was handy and could travel over most of the land without any trouble. When her friends came out to our farm, she often gave them a tour in the Jeep.

Although the Jeep got us around the farm easily, it had some mechanical problems. The gas tank rusted out, and the all-wheel drive transmission broke several times. As the years passed, the parts became harder to get. The radiator also started to leak badly one day during the summer when we were harvesting hay. The jeep was being used to pull wagons, so we would have to fill the radiator with water about every other trip to the barn. My hired man, Jake Medors, said that Red Man chewing tobacco would plug the leak and it would be as good as new. He put a pouch of chewing tobacco in the radiator, and we used it for a while. It started to overheat, and we found that the tobacco had plugged up the radiator so bad that we had to get a new one.

We kept the Jeep for about 10 years, but I became concerned about a person's safety while operating this vehicle. I had heard of accidents involving other Jeeps and the drivers had been killed. With these thoughts in mind, I sold the Jeep to a neighbor and he drove it for several more years. He replaced the transmission as we had done several times. Our family really enjoyed the jeep and it proved to be the handiest farm vehicle we ever owned. Our boys learned to drive using this vehicle and I still have many fond memories of the jeep.

Turkey Season

My cousin Isham Taft had been in the turkey-raising business his entire life. He learned the business from his mother who had raised turkeys most of her life. He seemed to have a skill at raising them and usually had about 150 birds for sale at Thanksgiving and Christmas. Each spring, Isham would go to Kilbourne, Illinois in Mason County to buy poults, which he would raise for market. It seems odd now, but the C& IM railroad raised baby turkeys and sold them to farmers. I guess they were trying to help the farmers establish themselves in the turkey business.

It became a tradition to help Isham during turkey season. We slaughtered the birds about three days prior to the respective holiday so they would be ready when people came for them. The work had to be done regardless of the weather. One year it rained all day. On another, there was ice coating everything. We had to improvise some creepers on our boots so we could move about. The turkey pen was a good city block from cousin Isham's house. At that time, he used his basement to slaughter and dress the birds. He would tell me what size of bird was desired, and it was my job to go to the turkey pen with a wire chicken catcher and catch a turkey that would weigh close to what the customer wanted. A hen turkey would weigh close to 16 pounds and a tom turkey would weigh from 18 to 22 pounds. This helped me determine which bird to catch. When the birds were ready for sale, they were sold at 65 cents a pound.

After I caught a bird, I had to carry it to the back of the house where there was an old stump and a wooden nail keg. We would put the bird on the stump and use a hatchet to cut the turkey's head off. Then we would put the bird in the nail keg to prevent it from flopping around and bruising itself. Next, we took the birds to the basement and scalded them in boiling hot water on the cooking stove. Then we would take the feathers off and clean the birds.

After the birds were prepared, we would weigh them and place a nametag on them for the customer. The tag would be tucked inside the turkey's leg, and we would place the prepared turkey in a water trough containing cool water and ice. Modern refrigeration methods were not available, so the icy water was the best way to keep the turkeys cool and preserved.

If the customer did not come to pick their turkey up, then it was my job to deliver the turkeys to the customers' homes. I delivered turkeys to Springfield, Rochester, Buckhart and the other local communities. I helped Isham from 1942 until 1950 when he decided to stop raising turkeys. He operated this business for many years and provided a good service to the public.

Signs of the Times

Home Medical Remedies

There were a number of home remedies that many people used in the early days to treat their ailments. Infections, embedded thorns, carbuncles, and ailments were often treated by applying some substance that would "draw out" the thorn or infection. One of the favorite ones that had widespread use was the application of a slice of raw bacon to the affected area. Some people said that this would draw so hard "that they could hardly stand the pain." Some others would argue that bread and sour milk would also draw out the poison.

Head lice were also a plague of some families during the early years. One method used to get rid of them, was to shave off all of the hair and rub kerosene on the scalp. Sometimes these individuals were called "onion heads." The kerosene would kill any lice eggs that still remained after most of the hair was shaved off.

Bed bugs were also dealt with using kerosene. All of the bed clothing was taken off of the mattress and it was wiped down or dapped with kerosene to kill all of the insects. After this treatment had been completed, it was wise not to smoke in bed.

Kerosene, or coal oil as it was known, was also used to treat colds. A little bit of kerosene was put on a teaspoon of sugar, and the sugar was swallowed. It is not known how successful this treatment proved to be.

Constipation was also dealt with using home remedies. One of the treatments for this ailment involved swallowing a lead bullet.

Because many of the children went barefooted, it was a common occurrence for them to step on a bee while walking about the yard. Bee stings were treated using baking soda mixed with a little water to form a paste. This was put on the sting and left in place until the pain had stopped.

Baking soda in water was also used to treat an upset stomach or heartburn. A teaspoon or two in a glass of water would often be enough to relieve the discomfort.

Bad chest colds were dealt with using onions fried in grease. The fried onions were placed on the chest of the sick person and covered with cheesecloth and rags. Then the person was wrapped in quilts. This procedure was repeated until the person was well once again. There are no available reports on the success of this method.

There were other methods of dealing with chest colds. When a goose was cooked, the grease or fat would be saved. In the winter, when a person developed a chest cold, the goose grease was heated, mixed with turpentine. Flannel was then soaked in the mixture and placed on the sick person's chest. Goose grease was no longer used when Vicks salve was developed.

Fried onions were also used to make what was known as a "Poultice". These were generally used to draw out some type of poison, such as a rattlesnake bite, an infection, a boil or carbuncle. As with the chest cold, the fried onions were wrapped in cheesecloth and placed on the affected area. The onions were supposed to draw the poison out of a person. When this happened, the onions would turn green. The sick person should then begin to feel better.

Sore throats were dealt with using salt water. A teaspoon of salt was mixed with a small glass of water and the sick person would gargle. The intent was to kill all of the germs with the salt. This remedy is still used by some people to this day.

There was also a remedy for anyone that might be stuck by one of the spines of a catfish while on a fishing trip. A big wad of freshly chewed tobacco was put on the wound. The wound may continue to sting for a while, but an infection rarely developed.

Tobacco was also used to treat ringworm. A cloth was soaked in the juice of tobacco and then placed on the infected area. This was kept on the infection for a few days and then removed. The tobacco usually killed the ringworm by the time the cloth was removed.

Old Time Recipes

Believe it or not, there was a time when it was a relatively common tradition for people to make pudding out of Suet. Suet is hard fat found in beef, similar to lard, which is found in pork. There is a long history of making suet pudding in the Taft Family. My mother used to make it on Thanksgiving and Christmas. Once the ingredients were combined, it had to cook for several hours in a double boiler. This pudding had to be cooked by the steam, not by direct contact with the heat. When it finished cooking, it was brown and had the texture of homemade bread. The pudding was served with a white sauce prepared separately.

The early Taft's made suet pudding regularly, so my grandfather asked Hoopie Smith, the local tinsmith, to make a special double boiler to make it in. The double boiler was made out of copper and was an engineering marvel. The lid of this boiler captured the steam and circulated it around the pudding until it was cooked. This Suet Pudding boiler became a family heirloom and was handed down from one generation to another.

Suet pudding was made during the fall and winter when a beef was butchered. It was likely we would have Suet Pudding for several weeks in a row because this was the time when suet was available. Although Suet Pudding was very good, many people today would say it is not very good for your cholesterol.

Taft Family steamer made by Hoopie Smith

Suet Pudding was made using two cups of finely chopped suet, two cups of stoned raisins, four cups of flour, two eggs, a pinch of salt, and enough milk to make a stiff batter. This mixture is then placed in a pudding bag and steamed for three hours. The sauce for the pudding includes one cup of sugar, one half cup of water, and yolk of one egg, one teaspoonful of butter, and one teaspoonful of flour. This mixture is flavored with lemon. This sauce is cooked in a saucepan at a low heat until the ingredients are thoroughly blended.

In the spring of the year, members of the Taft family would go outside and look for "Greens". Although there were several types of plants that could be used, their favorite was Sour Dock. The leaves of this plant were used to make a salad. The leaves were cut into small pieces and steamed. The steamed greens were flavored with a little vinegar. Vinegar was the only seasoning needed.

The spring was also the time when another favorite recipe was prepared, which was called "Skillet Pudding". This pudding was brown when finished, and it had a tendency to *fall* when baking. Falling would cause it to become rather rubbery and not very good to eat. My dad liked to eat this pudding after pouring clabbered milk, containing cinnamon on it. This dish was served when my mother served greens.

Christmas and Thanksgiving was also the time when we would have scalloped oysters. This is a tradition that has been in the Taft family for as long as we can remember. It is interesting to note that it is a long-standing tradition for people of Scottish descent to eat oysters for breakfast on Christmas morning. Because the Taft family comes from Scotland, perhaps our family tradition is connected to this old tradition.

Here are some old time recipes commonly prepared by the early settlers of Rochester.

Suet Pudding

1 cup of very finely chopped beef suet: ½ pound
Add gradually: 1 cup of sugar
When these ingredients are well blended, beat in: 3 egg yolks
Stir in: 1cup milk, 3 tablespoons brandy
Put through a grinder and add: 1-pound figs or dates or 2 cups peeled, sliced apples
Grate and add: 2 teaspoons orange rind, 1 teaspoon freshly ground nutmeg or ginger
Combine and add: 1 ½ cups dry bread crumbs, 2 teaspoons double-acting baking powder
Whip until stiff, then fold in: 3 egg whites
Pour the ingredients into a greased mold, steam slowly for four hours.
Serve with hot Sabayon sauce or Hot wine sauce
Flavor the sauce with 2 teaspoons or more of brandy

Strawberry Jam

One quart of hulled strawberries
Pour boiling water over strawberries and allow to stand 30 seconds
Drain water and add 2 cups of sugar and boil four minutes

Remove from heat and add 2 more cups of sugar
Boil four more minutes.
Let stand overnight. Put in jars and seal with wax.

Ice Cream

2 ½ cups of sugar1 quart of cream
Three eggs1 teaspoon of lemon extract
1-½ quarts of milk3 heaping tablespoons of cornstarch
Mix ½ cup of sugar with cornstarch. Dissolve with a little cold milk, and then add the beaten egg yolks. Heat the milk in a double boiler, then stir in the above mixture and add the rest of the sugar. Cook 15 minutes longer. Remove from fire and cool in freezer. Strain through cloth. Add cream, beaten egg white and flavoring. Finish filling freezer with milk and freeze. Cut ice from the horse trough if available. Makes 6 quarts.

Pickles

Fill a two-quart jar half full of pickles
Put in a piece of dill
Put in mixed spices
Put in a spoon of garlic
Put in a spoon of hot pepper
Put in a wine glass of vinegar
Fill jar with salt water

Boiled Soap

Two gallons of soft water
1 can of lye
Five pounds of strained grease
Boil slowly for two hours
Pour mixture in flat pan
Cut into cakes once cooled

Dandelion Wine

One gallon of blossoms
One gallon boiling water
Four oranges

Three lemons
Three pounds of sugar
½ cake of yeast
Pour water over blooms, let stand overnight
Squeeze all juice out of oranges and lemons
Strain blooms out of water
Put in two-gallon jug, add yeast, let stand for a few weeks

Springfield, Clear Lake and Rochester Railroad

Interurban railroads were a popular way to travel in the Springfield area during the early 1900s. Passengers traveled to picnics, Chautauqua's, swimming places and other recreation sites. Activities at Clear Lake and Glenwood Park attracted the attention of railroad personnel and investors, and Rochester was soon served by its own interurban rail system.

The Springfield, Clear Lake, and Rochester Railroad was incorporated on May 10, 1906. The intent was to construct an eight-mile line to Rochester plus a two and one-half mile branch line to the Chautauqua resort at Clear Lake. Plans were in place for an extension of the line from Rochester to Hillsboro. At Clear Lake, golfing, swimming, picnicking baseball, boating and other activities were planned. It was projected to become a haven for outdoor recreation activities.

The idea for a Chautauqua was promoted in the Springfield area, and financing was sought from local businessmen for the construction of the railroad. Grading of the line began on April 30, 1906 and track laying began later that same year. Six miles of track were in place by January 1, 1907 and on March 30, 1907, the first rail car operated on the line. The entire line was to be operated by electricity supplied from a site in Springfield. The railroad began services to the public on September 19, 1908 and charged fifteen cents for a ride to Springfield.

The railroad was plagued with problems from the beginning. Instead of using gravel for ballast like other railroads, the tracks were laid in dirt. There were problems with a weak power supply to trolleys farther from Springfield, causing them to go slower. Snow, frost, and sleet often brought the trolleys to a standstill, making it necessary for passengers to get out and push, especially at the grade near Clear Lake. During times of freezing rain, the motorman stood on top of the trolley and knocked ice off of the power wires with a broom while a passenger drove. On days like those, the trip from Rochester to Springfield could take as long as two hours.

Employees of the Railroad

There were other reasons why the trolleys took so long to make the trip. One trolley motorman used to have a loaded shotgun with him as he traveled between Springfield and Rochester, but it wasn't used to prevent robberies or other trouble. He used it to shoot rabbits as he traveled along the right-of-way, and he would stop and pick up those he killed and toss them into a basket he kept next to the gun. At the end of the day, it wasn't unusual for him to have a full basket of rabbits that he probably sold in Springfield.

These were not the only problems. The revenue from the operation of the railroad was not enough to pay the bills, including the money owed to the power company. The power company shut off the electricity. More bad news followed when a regulatory agency would not let the railroad operate until the tracks and bridges were made safe for travel. During this time when the trolleys were not operating, some men stole considerable amounts of the overhead wire used to operate the trains.

A group getting ready to go to Springfield from Uptown Rochester in front of the "Fanny Delay" grocery store

There was a Rochester businessman named Brown who had invested in the formation and operation of this railroad. Brown owned and operated the Rochester Bank. The operation of the railroad proved to be a big expense. When the railroad went bankrupt and was sold for junk in 1913, Brown's bank also went bankrupt. The Bell Family purchased the bank in 1912 and has operated it since then.

Although the railroad operated only six short years, it did provide much needed transportation between Rochester and Springfield. The resort at Clear Lake never materialized and neither did plans to extend the railroad to Hillsboro. If the upgrades and extensions of the railroad and the resort at Clear Lake had materialized, Rochester would have been a prominent stop on the railroad. The only visible remnant of

this railroad is the old rail bed near the Mechanicsburg Road east of
Springfield.

Then and Now

Many people often ask the question: "What is different about today
compared to the 1930s or 1940s. It would be easy to observe that
there are fast food stores in practically every town, more cars, more
people, computers and an abundance of cell phones. These are the
obvious differences, but there are many others few people recognize
or comprehend.

Kids aren't barefooted in the summer any longer. It was common for
most children, boys and girls, to go barefooted during these times.
Most parents could not afford to buy shores very often, and the kids
simply liked to go barefooted. With the coming of colder weather,
most people ordered shoes for their children from a catalog, like
Sears, Roebuck, and Company. The postman delivered mail items to
people's homes.

Horses are not used in farming any longer. Every farm had a stable or
livery barn to keep the draft horses in. The animals had to be fed and
watered several times each day. In order to go to the field, the horses
had to be harnessed and hitched to the implement to be used. During
this process, it was likely that the horse would run off, be contrary,
or step on your foot with its hoofs. This process had to be done four
times a day. First, in the morning, then before noon so the horses
could be fed, then they had to be re-hitched to go back to work and
finally un-hitched to be put away in the evening.

Harvesting the crop was very labor intensive. Shucking corn was all
done by hand instead of using a modern combine. Can you imagine
grabbing each ear of corn in the field, pulling it out of its husk with
a "shucking peg", and throwing it in a wagon pulled by a team of
horses. Each wagon held about 50 bushel. Not many men could shuck

2 wagons full per day. Then, the corn had to scooped out of the wagon and into the corncrib by hand using a number 12 steel scoop shovel.

Lard is no longer a staple in the kitchen. Lard was bought and sold at the local grocery store, and it was used to do the cooking by most farm families. Low fat oils have replaced lard, and very few families currently use it to fry meats and vegetables.

Few men chew tobacco today. It was very common for men to chew Red Man, Mickey Twist or Mail Pouch tobacco. Loose tobacco was sold in pouches, or individuals could buy what was called "plugs." The plug tobacco had been compressed and formed into a hard "cake." A knife would be used to cut the tobacco off for chewing. Every barbershop and some businesses had spittoons for their chewing customers. Today, most people below the age of forty have never seen a spittoon, let alone used one.

There were no interstate highways. The roads we did have were dirt, cinder or oil. Wet winter and spring month's often created nearly impassible conditions for automobiles. There were some two lane concrete highways that were called "hard roads" by the locals. The interstate system did not develop until President Eisenhower's Administration in the 1950s.

Airplanes are no longer made of cloth and wood. It was quite a common thing for most small planes during the 1920 and 1930s. The only metal parts on the aircraft were the engine, some wires and a few bolts. The cloth had to be painted so air would not pass through it. Any type of accident was devastating to these wood and cloth planes.

Pets now have doctors to take care of them. The development of veterinary science has greatly improved care for pets, but there were few veterinarians around during the 1930s. People also did not have money to spend for the care of their pets. Now there are operations and advanced care specifically for animals and that was unheard of during the early part of the last century. Also, pet food was not available in the stores. Dogs were fed leftovers from the table, and cats got some milk to drink at milking time. Otherwise, the cats hunted for mice in the barn or out in the fields. Now there are entire aisles in the stores filled with nothing but pet food in sacks, cans or pouches. Products like cat litter didn't exist, and no one thought of making treats for pets.

There have been many advances in our automobiles. We don't have to crank them any more, and they no longer have manual chokes to start them. There are steel-belted radials now instead of the thin old balloon tires that we used in the early years. Every car carried a hand pump and a tire repair kit because a flat tire was a near certainty on practically every trip.

Many people now say that they could not survive without the air conditioner. There were none in the 1920s and 1930s, so you could expect every store or place of business to be hot. The only things that we had to keep cool in the 1930s were a few small electric fans, crude devices by today's standards.

Most work, such as trenching or basement construction, was done by hand. There were no backhoes, power chain saws, weed eaters, power lawn mowers or other products like those in common use today.

Mail was picked up and delivered by trains instead of by truck. When the train picked up the mail, it didn't stop. The trains coming through the area might slow for the mail, but they wouldn't stop. The post office workers would have to sling the bags of mail into an open door of a moving car as it rolled along in front of the train depot. Later, the trains using an arm on the train that would hook the mail sacks as it went by picked up mail sacks. Postal clerks sorted the mail while on the trains. They had to know every town and village in the area because there were no zip codes. If a letter was mailed in Rochester and was to be delivered in Edinburg, the mail clerk would have to sort the mail and get the Edinburg mail ready to be offloaded by the time the train got to Edinburg, which was the next town down the line.

Entertainment and communication have changed dramatically. In the 1930s, no one had heard of television. In the early 1950s when televisions first appeared in some homes, many neighbors would come over and watch the programs for hours. There were no compact discs or video players. There were no portable radios and no boom boxes. Practically everyone has a cell phone today, but when I was growing up, people were just glad to have one party-line telephone in their home.

It was also much easier to get building projects completed in the early years. During those times, no one developed detailed drawings, applied for permits or dealt with all of the regulations that are required in today's world. The completion of many projects is now much more complicated and expensive. The entire process reminds me of a story that I recently encountered:

"It is the year 2003 and Noah lives in the United States.

The Lord spoke to Noah and said: "In one year I am going to make it rain and cover the whole earth with water until all is destroyed. I want you to save the righteous people and two of every kind of living thing on the earth. Therefore, I am commanding you to build an ark."

"Remember," said the Lord, "You must complete the ark and bring everything aboard in one year."

Exactly one year later, a fierce storm cloud covered the earth, and all the seas of the earth went into tumult. The Lord saw Noah sitting in his front yard weeping.

"Noah," he said, "Where is the ark?"

Lord please forgive me!" cried Noah. I did my best, but there were big problems. First, I had to get a permit for construction and your plans did not comply with the codes. I had to hire an engineering firm and redraw the plans.

Then I got into a fight with OSHA over whether or not the Ark needed a fire sprinkler system and floatation devices. Then my neighbor objected, claiming I was violating zoning ordnances by building the ark in my front yard, so I had to get a variance from the city planning commission.

I had problems getting enough wood for the ark because there was a ban on cutting trees to protect the spotted owl. I finally convinced the U. S. Forest Service that I needed the wood to save the owls, however the Fish and Wildlife Service won't let me catch any owls, so no owls.

The carpenters formed a union and went out on strike. I had to negotiate a settlement with the National Labor Union. Now I have 16 carpenters on the ark, but still no owls.

When I started rounding up the other animals, an animal rights group sued me. They objected to me only taking two of each kind aboard. Just when I got the suit dismissed, the EPA notified me that I could not complete the ark without filing an environmental impact statement on your proposed flood. They didn't take very kindly to the idea that they had no jurisdiction over the conduct of the creator of the universe.

Then the Army Corps of Engineers demanded a map of the proposed new flood plain. I sent them a globe. Right now, I am trying to resolve a complaint filed with Equal Employment Opportunity Commission that I am practicing discrimination by not taking, godless, unbelieving people aboard!

The IRS has seized all of my assets, claiming that I'm building the ark in preparation to flee the country to avoid paying taxes. I just got a notice from the State that I owe some kind of user tax and failed to register the ark as a recreational watercraft. Finally, the ACLU got the courts to issue an injunction against further construction of the ark, saying that since God is flooding the earth, it is a religious event and therefore unconstitutional.

"I really don't think I can finish the ark for another five or six years." Noah replied.

The sky began to clear, and the sun began to shine and seas began to calm. A rainbow arched across the sky. Noah looked up hopefully. You mean you are not going to destroy the earth, Lord?

"No." said the Lord sadly." The government already has."

Adventures

The Interurban and the Swift Chicken Truck

During the first half of the last century, most every little town had a person who sold and bought chickens. Many of these individuals worked for the Swift Packing Company, with its headquarters located at "Union Stockyards" in Chicago. In Rochester, Jess Fowler was the Swift Chicken representative. His truck could be seen practically every day hauling chickens to Springfield or going out into the country to buy chickens.

The Swift Chicken representatives would come to your farm and select chickens to buy. He would also give advice on care and feeding of chickens, and he provided a valuable service to the farm community. During those days, nearly every farm had chickens.

Chickens were transported in wooden crates. They had wooden spokes along the outside that were spaced close together so the chickens couldn't get out. These wooden crates were stacked on top of each other when they were full. Sometimes they were stacked up to six crates high. Ropes were used to tie the crates in place so they would not fall off when the truck was moving. The trucks did not have any sideboards, because they would have made the loading and unloading of the chickens more difficult.

I was going to school at the University of Illinois during the winter of 1942. Christmas vacation had just ended, and I had to return to campus. It was January and it had recently stormed. There was a layer of snow and ice on the roads. During those days, a trip from Springfield to Champaign was regarded as a very long trip, and few people drove that far. My dad took me to the Interurban depot in Springfield so I could travel by train. This railroad operated between Springfield and

117

Champaign at that time.

I boarded the train and we were traveling along without any trouble until we got to the countryside near Bement, east of Decatur. At that point, it was dark, but I could see a Swift Chicken truck moving along a road that crossed the tracks. It was trying to stop to allow the train to pass. Due to the slick road, the truck continued to slide onto the tracks in front of the approaching train.

The train engineer saw the truck and applied the brakes, but he could not get the train to stop before hitting the truck. The train was almost stopped at the moment of impact, but the train's momentum shoved the truck off of the tracks and several crates of chickens fell to the ground.

No one was hurt by the collision, and no damage was done to the train or the truck. Several chicken crates were damaged and about fifteen chickens were clucking and trying to walk through the foot-deep snow. I got off of the train with the conductor. With a few other farm boys, we managed to catch all of the chickens and helped put them back into the crates. Once they were tied down securely, we pushed the truck back onto the road. The grateful driver drove away with his load of chickens, with only minimal damage to a few crates.

We boarded the train and resumed our trip to Champaign without any other incidents. As far as I know, there was no damage accident report filed and not one police or other emergency vehicle came to the scene. In contrast to today, it would likely be hours before the truck and train could be underway again, and all sorts of emergency vehicles and personnel would be called to the scene.

School Boy Tricks

We were no different from other boys when it came to playing tricks on people at school. If a new idea presented itself, we were sure to take advantage of it. We learned a new trick from some coal miners that were fishing on the South Fork River one summer, during the Great Depression. This became one of our favorites.

It was carbide. The coal miners used it in their lights while fishing at night, and they showed us how it produced a gas when combined with water. We were fascinated. One of us came up with the idea to take some to school and put it in inkwells that belonged to the girls. The carbide would react with the ink and produce a gas that would blow the lid off the ink well. Ink would fly everywhere, even to the ceiling of the room. There were very few weeks when an inkwell didn't blow up. We thought it was great fun.

Our teacher didn't think there was anything funny about the explosions. Her method of dealing with the problem was to have all of the boys line up along the side of the classroom. Then she would reach into our pockets and take out all of the carbide crystals. We didn't like losing our carbide to the teacher. One of my friends really didn't like losing his. He was a couple of years older than the rest of us because he had flunked twice. One day he said he was going to teach her a lesson that she would not soon forget. The next morning, he came to school without any underwear on and had cut out the bottom of his pants pockets, where he normally kept his carbide. As expected, the teacher lined us up so she could search us. You can imagine what happened when our teacher reached into his pocket looking for carbide! She had a very surprised look on her face. Needless to say, there were no more searches for carbide, and inkwells continued to blow up.

There was a day when I was in high school when we found a dead skunk. We took the skunk to school and put it in a locker. It wasn't long before the fragrance was throughout the building, and the teachers were looking for the source of the smell. When they finally found the skunk, no one had any idea how the skunk got into the locker.

One of our school tricks started out as a Halloween prank. Most local people had milk cows in those days, and one of my friends had one at his house, which was close to the school. We got the idea that we would take the cow and put her in the school. About 9:00 P.M we lead the cow to the school. We managed to open the front door, so we took the cow inside, closed the door, and took off running toward our homes. The following morning, the janitor found to his surprise a cow walking around in the school. She had left a number of calling cards on the hallway floors.

One wall in our room had a big Seth Thomas wall clock on it that was used to regulate the time for school activities. One of the daily activities involved ringing the bell for lunch at noon, for recess, and for the closing of school for the day. The button switch to ring the bell was located in our coatroom, and one of the girls was often asked to go ring the bell at the appropriate time. We soon developed some tricks to play with the clock and the bell. When our teacher was out of the room, one of us would stand on the shoulders of one of the older boys and we would move the clock hand back during the noon break or at recess so our free time would be longer. If the end of school were near, we would move the clock hand forward so school would be dismissed early.

We also had a large globe of the earth hanging from the ceiling that could be raised or lowered by a rope, which was attached to a weight located on one side of the room. I would get close to the blackboard where the rope used to raise and lower the globe was located. When our teacher was working with one of the other classes in our room, I would use the rope to lower the globe until it was about to touch her head. She was totally unaware this was happening. I would keep this up until the laughter got so loud that she would look around and catch me. She would grab me, throw me over the piano bench, and spank me with this big paddle she kept in her desk. There were few days that she didn't spank me at least three times.

That caused me to start thinking about how we could get rid of that paddle. Her nephew had made the paddle she used on me and the other boys. It was big and sturdy with lots of holes in the flat part to make it hurt more. My chance came one day when she was out of the room. Several of us boys went to her desk, got the paddle, and managed to sneak it out of the school. During recess, we put it down in the hole of the boys outside toilet. It was gone the next time she looked for it. When she asked us about the paddle, all of us said that we had no idea what happened to it, and were surprised to learn that it was gone.

The boy's outdoor toilet was the scene of another trick. The toilet had an outside vent, about ten inches in diameter, located along the middle of the back wall that opened to the pits below ground. It was a very windy day in March. When the wind blew especially strong, the wind would whistle up through the bottom of the toilet and out through the vent. Although we normally had a roll of tissue paper hanging on the wall, the janitor got several bundles of tissue paper that came in individual sheets. I got the idea to put a handful of these tissues down into the pit under the opening for the vent. The suction created by the wind would carry these out of the top of the toilet and onto the schoolyard. Several of us did this throughout the day, and tissues were scattered all over the schoolyard. When we were questioned, we explained that the wind was sucking the used tissue up the vent and blowing it over the schoolyard.

I've often thought of the fire hazard we boys made by leaving newspapers in the crawl space, under the grade school. It was customary to bring our lunch wrapped in newspaper every day. We would crawl through an open vent screen and into the crawl space under the school to eat lunch. It was normally nice and warm there. We would just leave the newspaper after finishing lunch. After our grade school careers, their was a lot of newspapers in the crawl space.

We don't know what ever happened to all of them. Now, as an adult, leaving all those papers was not such a good idea.

Ironically, despite all the tricks during my school years, I was elected to the school board and was chosen president in the 1950s, when I was 32 years old.

A Visit to Gobbler's Knob

Deep in the timber, not far from Glenwood Park, was a place known as Gobbler's Knob. There was a building there that was built on stilts that was used as a drinking and dance hall for many years. The building was built of rough-sawed lumber from a local sawmill. There was nothing fancy about the construction and people didn't care about the appearance of the building. They were out to have some fun. This was the Great Depression, and few people had much money.

Gobblers Knob was in the woods about three miles north of Rochester, just past the location where Black Branch joins the South Fork River. There was a covered bridge over Black Branch during earlier years, but it was gone before the days of Gobbler's Knob.

The music each evening was provided by a local band. They would have a fiddle, banjo, and guitar, and one of the band members usually could sing a few songs. That was all that was needed for the crowd to get out on the dance floor. They served beer at this place, and probably some bathtub gin. There were no roads or paths to this place, but people drove their cars to the nearest road, parked their cars, and walked the rest of the way.

Carl Young had told me about Gobbler's Knob at school. He thought that we should go there some night. One night when I was about eight years old, Carl and I rode our ponies to Gobbler's Knob. He had convinced me that we should go. My parents knew that I was going to the Young's, but they didn't know what our plans were for that night.

We waited until it was dark and the dancing had started. We tied our ponies behind the building once we arrived and went inside. What an awakening!

We were both in the third grade, and neither one of us had ever been to a dance hall or seen a keg of beer. We sat down in some old chairs, and I noticed an old tin cup hanging from a nail on one of the walls. It was one of the beer drinking cups. No one was paying any attention to us, so I went over and got that tin cup, filled it with beer, and drank it. Carl soon thought that he would try one. After we finished our beer, we sat around watching the people dance. We left the place after about 45 minutes and started on our way home.

I do remember being a little dizzy on the way back home, and it wasn't very pleasant. The jiggling from the horse ride didn't help the situation at all. It was a good thing that my parents were in bed asleep. That one trip was enough for me. I never went back to Gobbler's Knob.

Gobbler's Knob has been gone for many years now. No one is quite sure when the building disappeared, but it is likely that the big flood of 1943 destroyed it. The building was entirely within the floodplain and 1943 was the biggest flood that any one remembers.

Politics

First on the Ballot

I took the occasion of my daughters 38th birthday to write a little of my political history, for I was 38 years old in the year of these events. I had already served as president of the Rochester School Board. Then I was elected to my first political office, Township Supervisor, and member of the County Board of Supervisors of Sangamon County.

Front row, left to right: George Drack, Robert Conn, Author, Josephine Oblinger. Back row: Scottie Hinton, Judge William Conway, Judge Stanley Thomas, Senator from Chicago, W.C. "Bill" Schaffer.

In February of 1962, I was selected as best qualified to be the Republican candidate for the office of Clerk of the Probate Court for the county. Also chosen was Bill Schaffer for Sheriff, George Erickson for County Treasurer, and Josephine Oblinger as County Clerk. The first to file at 8:00 o'clock on this morning would be first on the "Republican Primary Election" ballot, which was where everyone wanted to be. We all felt the competition.

We three men decided that we should be in line at the courthouse door by midnight the night before, therefore establishing our position. It was a cold night, and after about an hour outside, the Sheriff, Hugh Campbell, who was custodian of the courthouse, came to us and said, "Ascertain your positions and come on in the building to stay warm." This was much appreciated by all.

Not long after being inside, two men, who were Democrats, desiring to be candidates for Sheriff came in the building. Soon after their arrival, an awful argument started as to who was first in line. Hugh Campbell, also a Democrat, told them that he had a plan to settle the argument. Both of these men were young city policemen and were real macho types. The plan was to allow them to race up the three flights of stairs to the third floor. The sheriff stationed himself at the top, so as to declare a winner, and had one of his deputies at the lower level start the race. Well, I never saw such a scramble. They fought one another on hands and knees all the way up. A winner was declared for the first and second positions on the ballot. What a way to run politics. The irony of this is that another man came in and filed for the Democratic primary for sheriff and won the election. This man, James Christianson, was elected sheriff in the fall election.

Well, I won the fall election and was sworn in as the Probate Clerk of Sangamon County on December 3, 1962. I was very proud to introduce that day, my wife and five children. The youngest, Miss Carolyn Mardell, was having her first birthday that very day.

The day I was sworn in and Carolyn's first birthday

Tales from the Sheriffs Office

Once my term as Probate Clerk was up in 1966, the newly elected sheriff, Eddie Ryan, asked if I wanted to be his under sheriff. This would prove to be a most interesting job.

During this work, we issued all kinds of civil papers. For instance, we were involved in a situation where two girls co-owned furniture in an apartment. There had been some changes in their lives, and one of them was now locked out and her furniture was still in the apartment. I asked her: "Do you have a way of hauling the furniture if we can get into the apartment? If she said yes, I would ask her to meet us there at a specified hour on a certain day. I would send one of my biggest, toughest-looking deputies to the place, and load the furniture that she said she owned. The other party would complain, but we told her she should have given her roommate what was rightfully hers in

127

the beginning. As I look back, I am not sure that this method was completely legal, but it sure solved the problem in a hurry.

Some of the more challenging work involved murder cases. I do not consider myself to be a great detective, but I was written up twice in *True Detective*, a magazine devoted to police work. One story involved a crime that became known as: "The Missing Head". The crime began at a nightclub in Springfield and involved a handyman who worked for the club owner. The handyman rented a single room apartment owned by the club owner. These two men had a dispute over the rent. Additionally, the club owner often ridiculed the handyman, calling him "retarded". The club owner ordered him to vacate his apartment. When the club owner came to evict him, an argument started and the owner was shot and killed with a shotgun. However, the owner had not traveled to the apartment alone. Another man was waiting in the truck, and when his friend did not return, he went to find out why. When he discovered the club owner dead, the handyman killed him with the shotgun too. Now he had two bodies on his hands.

The shells used to kill the two men had been reloaded. This may have caused him to come up with the idea that no one could trace the murders back to him if he cut out the shot that was in the bodies. He dismembered the bodies and buried some of the parts in a posthole, south of Springfield. He took the rest of the body parts to Meredosia and threw them off the bridge into the Illinois River. On the way back to Springfield, he crashed the truck, which was owned by the murdered club owner, into a utility pole on Route 36 near New Berlin. The truck caught on fire, so he abandoned it and walked back to Springfield on the railroad. The police discovered the burning truck plus several bloody boxes that were still in the bed of the truck.

Our first indication of foul play was a phone call from some mushroom hunters who informed us they had found some cut up body part in a posthole. We then learned of the crashed pick-up truck on route 36, and through license plate identification, found the owner to be the nightclub owner. We called the mother of the nightclub owner and asked her if she had seen her son. She had not, but she did say he was going to see his handyman who had been causing him a lot of trouble. We went to the handyman's place and found him sitting on top of the building, holding a shotgun. We told him not to shoot because we would shoot him if he did. He let us approach the building and then came down from the roof. We found blood everywhere inside the building, and on some sand he had used to try to clean the place. His fingernails also had blood and grease under them, like someone that had recently been butchering a hog. We suspected he had not cleaned his hands since he butchered the two men.

We put the handcuffs on him and took him to jail. He never said a word then or throughout the entire trial. He was convicted and is serving a life sentence. We found many of the body parts in the posthole and along the Illinois River, but the head of one victim was never found.

The second murder trial, described in *True Detective*, involved a businessman from Springfield. A tow truck was called shortly after midnight, to come after a car that was stranded along a muddy road East of Springfield. The tow truck driver could not find the car, but he did find a man standing along the road. He had been shot and was holding onto a post for support. He had lost a lot of blood.

The truck driver took him back to Springfield. The injured man was operated on at Memorial Hospital, but died not long afterwards. Now it was a murder, and it soon developed into an interesting case.

Later that evening a deputy sheriff found a car in Lincoln Park, near the lagoon, with a man asleep inside, and blood all over the seat. The situation looked very suspicious, so the deputy arrested the man and took him to jail. The car proved to belong to the victim who had died.

The sheriff suggested the murder weapon might be in the Lincoln Park

Lagoon. He wanted to get the fire department to pump the lagoon dry so the gun could be found. At that moment, a young boy rode by on his bicycle. He stopped and asked what we were looking for. When he learned that we were looking for a gun, he said that he had found one under the bridge over the lagoon. We went with him to his home, but learned his dad had taken the gun with him to work at Pillsbury Mills. We went to Pillsbury Mills where we found his dad and retrieved the gun.

I learned the suspect had stayed at the Capitol Hotel, so I went to his room. The bed had not been made, and there was a peculiar black mark on the bedclothes that looked like gunpowder. Upon examining the floor, we found a bullet hole. After extracting this bullet, we found that it matched the bullets taken from the body. The same gun fired the bullets, which killed the victim, and made the hole in the floor of the hotel room.

We brought the accused man to trial and he was found guilty of murder and sentenced to life in prison. I have since learned he has been the shortstop on the Menard Correctional Center's baseball team for many years. Before the crime, he had been on his way to Florida to try out for the St. Louis Cardinals.

Transporting Prisoners

During my time with the Sangamon County Sheriff's Department, I traveled to several states to pick up, or extradite prisoners who had been arrested and were being held in other jurisdictions. My usual method of travel was by squad car, and the trips were often long and tiring.

I made a trip to Pensacola, Florida once to pick up a man who had been arrested by the local police. I arrived in town, made my way to the jail and soon had the prisoner cuffed and in chains, ready for the trip back home. Before we left town, the man asked me: "Mr. Taft, I have been in that jail for 30 days and the only things I have had to eat has been mush for breakfast, beans for lunch and both of them mixed together for dinner. I have been eating this jail food for a long time, and it doesn't set well on my stomach. If you could find a place, would it be possible for you to get a cheeseburger for me to eat". After finding a place that served hamburgers, I stopped and got one for him. That left a lasting impression on me. That fellow was more concerned about eating a greasy burger than he was about going back to Springfield to face trial.

The author manning the FBI booth at the State Fair

I was in Tennessee on another trip when I came upon an automobile accident. A woman was impatient and wanted to get around the cars. She asked me to direct traffic so she could leave. I told her I didn't know anything about the traffic laws of Tennessee and very little about those of Illinois. The local officer was doing just fine and did not need any help. You see everything when you are on the highways of America.

On another trip, I went to Jackson, Mississippi to get a prisoner. As I drove through town looking for the jail, I came upon a city police officer directing traffic at a busy intersection. I stopped and asked for directions to the county jail and he replied: "Wait a moment and I will show you the way." It wasn't long before he was in the car with me and we were headed to the jail. I thought it was a little unusual for him to stop his traffic assignment and ride with me, but it was nice of him. I guess it was an example of Southern hospitality, or he hated traffic duty.

I was in Utah on another trip to pick up a prisoner. When I arrived, the local officials informed me they were holding a second inmate who was wanted in Springfield. I phoned the state's attorney to see if it would be all right to return with both men. I was asked if I could handle both prisoners, and I replied that I thought I could.

After talking with the local sheriff, I learned that these two desperado's had held up a local gas station and were subsequently captured. This was a very small town, and it was apparent every-one knew every-one else. The sheriff referred to the gas station owner by name just like he did the proprietors of the other town businesses. They seemed quite chummy.

As I was preparing to leave, the local sheriff appeared with two envelopes containing the prisoner's personal belongings. He opened them and took out wallets containing around $600. Then, he called the gas station owner and asked him how much was stolen from him in the robbery. The owner said he would be right down. When he got there, he told the sheriff that he was missing $140. The sheriff peeled $140 from the wallets and handed it to the gas station owner.

Then, he put the remaining money in his pocket. After that, he handed me their empty wallets. The Sheriff kept the rest, about $440, and two televisions that they had stolen. The two prisoners complained about the sheriff keeping their money and televisions but it didn't do any good. The sheriff made out pretty well. I guess you could say, "western justice was served".

These two prisoners got along very well on the trip back home. I learned that they were both from Springfield and knew each other very well. In fact, they had gone to Utah together and had planned and completed several robberies. They pointed out businesses in Kansas and Utah that they had robbed while we were driving back home.

The weather was a little uncertain when I left. By the time I reached Loveland Pass, I was in the worst snowstorm I had ever seen. The snow was soon so deep that the car couldn't make any progress. I knew there were chains in the trunk, and I tried to put them on by myself. I didn't have any luck, so the prisoners said they could put the chains on for me. I let them out, took their cuffs off and let them try to put the chains on the tires. They didn't have any coats; hats or gloves and they were not prepared to be outside. I had my pistol and stood back from them as they worked. They tried to put the chains on the tires, but didn't have any better luck than I did, so I put the cuffs on them and put them back in the car. Now I had no choice but to turn around and find a service station.

A local service station put the tire chains on, and I did not have any more trouble getting through the snow. I drove through all that snow and was well on the other side of the mountain before I had the chains taken off. I never would have made it through the snow without the chains, and the money spent to have them installed was well worth it. This took place during the last week of October in 1967. Considering the weather and the fact that I was returning home with two prisoners, it was a very pleasant trip. I learned that these men were proud of the robberies that they had committed and laughed about what they had done.

They were very friendly and I had to remind myself that they were prisoners and not friends of mine. The ironic thing was that they were promptly acquitted when the trial began. A positive identification of the suspects could not be made. I am sure they got a laugh out of being acquitted, just like they laughed about the string of robberies that they committed in Utah and Kansas.

Bits of Political Wisdom

Abraham Lincoln said that it didn't matter how good a person's ideas and integrity were if they didn't get elected to office. That was the most important first step in a person's political career. Once they were elected, then they would have the opportunity to put their ideas to work and their integrity into practice. I remembered that when I was running for political office.

The author chats with his Bill Scott, Attorney General of Illinois

Interest in political life goes back many years in the Taft Family. My great, great grandfather, Josiah Taft, served two terms in the

Vermont General Assembly, and many of the family members were active in local political life. This interest continued when the family moved to Illinois in the 1820s. My grandfather and father served on the Rochester School Board and were active in community service. Discussion in our house centered on local issues much of the time, and when I was older, I joined in on these discussions. As I matured, I became more interested in community activities, and was naturally drawn into public life.

I felt that in order to be honest to any future constituency, a candidate for public office must feel an obligation of high moral character and uncompromising effort while serving. I think this was demonstrated during the time I was asked to be the campaign chairperson for the Red Cross, March of Dimes, and the American Cancer Society. It would have been easy to say that I was too busy, but these were very worthwhile activities and were deserving of my time. It wasn't that I had more time than others; I felt an obligation to work on these projects. This is the same approach that I took to political life when I ran for and was elected to many offices during the next twenty years.

The first lesson in politics is name recognition. If people didn't know who you were, it wasn't very likely that you would win. I tried to get people to remember me in various ways, but my favorite was the horse and wagon. I took the horse and wagon to Springfield and drove it through the streets. My message, written on signs hanging on the sides of the wagon was: "Let's put Horse Sense Back into Government." Lots of people commented that they remembered me as the candidate who promised to put common sense back into government operations.

Another lesson I leaned early was, you couldn't take to heart what everyone tells you. When I ran for Township Supervisor, I talked to everyone in the township and every one of them said they were going to vote for me. I won the election by seven votes. Politics could be very fickle.

135

Some of the best advice that I ever received came from a man named Robert Rees. His advice was to get the audience involved in your speech by asking questions, which have an obvious answer. If you could do that, then the chances were good that they would remember you and vote for you at election time. This proved to be very valuable advice. Candidates would travel together when they were on the campaign trail, and it wasn't unusual for four or five candidates to travel together. We would always be addressing a Republican crowd, so the first speaker, who usually was me, would ask the question:" Do you believe we should elect Richard Nixon as president of the United States?" The crowd would answer with a loud "yes", so the next question was: "Should we elect Richard Ogilvie governor of Illinois?" There would be another thunderous "yes" from the crowd.

I would ask the question: "Do you believe the Democrats are causing too much inflation?" The answer would be a loud "yes". When I was in farming country I would say that a haircut used to cost a bushel of corn. Now, inflation is so bad, it costs four bushels of corn. This is what the democrats have done to us.

When I was in Chicago or another large city, I used stories of people coming from rural backgrounds. "I bet that most of you are about two or three generations removed from the farm, and you wished you were back." People would come up to me and tell me they remembered their grandfather's farm or some other relative's farm as it was in their childhood. They did wish they were back on the farm.

I would also use the story of when I was a child about ten. "When I made my first dollar, I went to the store to buy a picture frame so I could frame it. I spent ten cents on the frame for the dollar. Today, the picture frame would cost you a dollar and the dollar that you frame is worth ten cents." This is the inflation that the democrats have created.

I would also tell the crowds that "The only way we Republicans could do anything about this inflation is to speak up and vote. I am reminded of a story about a man who bought his wife a parrot that was so smart, he could speak three languages. His wife had always wanted a parrot, and he thought one that could speak three languages would make a wonderful present. He had the parrot delivered to their home, and couldn't wait until it was time for him to leave work. When he arrived home, he asked about the parrot and told his wife that he could speak three languages. His wife replied that the parrot never said anything, so she had prepared him for her birthday meal. He was now roasting in the oven." I would follow up this story with: "If we don't speak up and vote, things are not going to change, and we could end up like the parrot."

I would tell another story about how we had to be careful and recognize what these liberal democrats were doing. They slowly make changes, which appear to be rather uneventful at first, but the end result is not good. Then I would tell the story of the pigs that ran wild in the woods, and no one could catch them. A liberal democrat came along and said that he could catch them. He put out some corn the next day, and by the next day the corn was gone. Greater amounts of corn were brought in each day until the pigs became used to feeding on the corn at this spot. Then he started to build a fence. The pigs didn't pay any attention. It wasn't long before he had a fence built completely around the area, and the pigs were coming in to feed through the gate. Late one night when the pigs were eating, the man closed the gate. This is what the liberal democrats are doing by changing things little by little until the gate closes and we are caught inside.

I always presented myself as an honest sincere candidate, interested in doing a good job for the people. I spent more money making sure my record was clean and clear than I ever took in from political contributors.

On the Campaign Trail

One of the best experiences I had on any campaign occurred during the 1968 campaign for Clerk of the Illinois Supreme Court. A "Whistle Stop" train tour was organized by the Ogilvie for Governor people. All of the statewide candidates were aboard, plus representatives from the Nixon for President campaign.

The train was donated by one of the big wealthy families from Chicago. The train had a Pullman car, a dining car that had a platform on the end, plus the locomotive.

The "Republican Victory Special" as it pulls out of Springfield

The republican candidates riding the train were Everett Dirksen for U. S. Senator, Richard Ogilvie for Governor, Bill Harris for Comptroller, Bill Scott for Treasurer, and Don Carpentier for Secretary of State, and I was running for Clerk of the Supreme Court. David Eisenhower and Julie Nixon came to Illinois and rode on the train with us for an entire day.

We traveled 1700 miles by rail over the space of three days. We had to change locomotives whenever we went from one railroad Company to another. There were also times when we traveled on tracks that that had not been used for over a year. We had to go pretty slow on these tracks, but we never had any big trouble. The railroads seemed to know what they were doing.

We made seventeen stops one day, and we each gave about 15 speeches. We usually spoke from the platform on the back of the last car. We stopped in Danville, Champaign, Galesburg, Pontiac, and went as far south as Carbondale. Local dignities would often join us on the train and ride with us until the next stop. There would be 15 to 20 new individuals that would join us at practically every stop. They would arrange for someone to pick them up and take them back home.

I was usually was the first to speak when we arrived at a new stop. After speaking, I would go out into the crowd to greet the people. It was always good to meet the people in person.

Elected Offices

As an adult, I had always done volunteer work for the Red Cross and other organizations in the community. People seemed to appreciate my efforts, and some individuals began to encourage me to run for the Rochester School Board. I gave it some thought, and in 1955, I did run for the school board. It was the first elected office I had ever sought.

I did a little campaigning, but relied mostly on people knowing what I had done in Rochester. The election was held in April and I received enough votes to gain a place on the school board. I was very pleased to serve because I have always believed the school board was a very important part of the community.

I was elected president of the school board during my second year. Rochester was starting to grow and we began a building program to accommodate that growth. As President of the school board, I believed it was important to lead on issues involving the school. It was decided a bond issue was needed, and several meetings were held where I explained the need for a new high school to several different community organizations. It was a lot of work, and I learned a lot about local government, bond issues, and tax rates. The bond issue passed overwhelmingly.

In 1958, I ran on the Republican ticket for township supervisor and was elected. My job was to take care of the needy, and serve as the treasurer, and general supervisor of the township. There weren't many families in need of financial assistance in those days.

My position as supervisor also meant I was a member of the Sangamon County Board. While I was a board member, we sold the old county courthouse to the State of Illinois for $600,000. This is the same courthouse made famous by Abe Lincoln's "House Divided" speech.

I was appointed to a committee regarding activities related to coal mines, but there was only one mine in the entire county at the time. We learned the state was already involved in the same type of work, so we decided there was no longer a need for a committee of this type. We soon learned there was a need for a committee to look at countywide zoning. Practically every town, including Rochester, was beginning to grow, and we believed there should be someone to regulate development. I was a member of this committee and this work proved to be very interesting.

One of the concepts developed was greenbelts along streams. Under this concept, grasses or trees would be planted along streams to prevent erosion. No homes could be built in these greenbelts due to the likelihood of flooding. This concept was not well received at the time, and no greenbelts were developed in the county. This same concept is being discussed today with greater public support.

The fall election of 1962 brought change to political offices in Illinois.

That was the year I was elected Probate Clerk of Sangamon County. A judicial amendment to the Illinois Constitution was approved in the same election. It consolidated the Probate Clerk's office into the office of the Circuit Clerk. This did not prohibit me from serving my term of four years as Probate Clerk, but meant there would be no possibility of re-election. There were many other changes that took place, including elimination of the old justice of the peace and police magistrates. These changes also provided for the election of two more circuit judges in Sangamon County.

The fall of 1965 also brought big changes. We had to move from the old courthouse, located on the downtown square of Springfield, to a new county building located at Eighth and Monroe. This new county building was out grown after only 20 years. The short life of this building is tribute to the rapid growth of Sangamon County and it's communities. A new one built in the 1990's, now serves the needs of the county.

I served for four years in the county building as the Probate Clerk. It is interesting to note that the first probate clerk, Frank Harcourt, was from Rochester. Due to the changes that took place with the passage of new laws in 1962, I was the last probate clerk, also from Rochester. There were numerous probate clerks between Frank Harcourt and me, but none of them were from Rochester.

During my tenure as probate clerk, we handled over 1,000 probate estates, 300 guardianships, and 300 conservatorships per year. We took care of business for people who could not take care of themselves.

One of the interesting events that took place while I was Probate Clerk was a visit and talk given by Ulysses S. Grant IV. He spoke to the Sangamon County Historical Society in the probate courtroom where his great grandfather, General and President Ulysses S. Grant, was sworn into service during the Civil war.

Ulysses S. Grant IV was about 65 years old at the time of this event. Like his grandfather, he was a graduate of West Point, and was a very distinguished gentleman. He was retired from the Army and was living in Virginia.

Another interesting aspect of the work as Probate Clerk was the large number of contacts with people doing genealogical work. The county's old records were kept in file boxes, wrapped in paper and tied with a ribbon. We would look up the file for a particular family and help them research their family records.

After my term as Probate Clerk, I accepted a job offer from the newly elected Sheriff, Eddie Ryan. I really enjoyed my years there, but I became interested in being Clerk of the Supreme Court of Illinois. I was aware there might be a vacancy because the incumbent clerk was in poor health. One of my initial problems was to get on the state wide Primary Ballot. The deadline to file petitions was only two days away when I decided to run. I needed petitions with 3,000 signatures in order to file. A friend printed petitions for me, and several Sheriff's deputies and numerous volunteers took them and started getting signatures. One of the best places for signatures was at taverns where plenty of people could be found. We even took some to the Morgan County Sheriff whose deputies took them around to taverns in their county.

We worked day and night on the petitions and finally finished them at 5:00 on the last day. I had the 3,000 signatures needed and I was on the ballot with two other people. I won the primary election and became the Republican candidate for Clerk of the Supreme Court in the November 1968 general election.

Running in a statewide general election in Illinois is a grueling, time-consuming endeavor. It was in 1968 and is true today. I took one of my personal cars and had my name and the office I was running for painted on both sides. I drove it over 20,000 miles and spoke at over 50 courthouses in the counties of Illinois. We also took a great "Whistle

Stop" train ride as described in *On the Campaign Trail.* Our downstate headquarters was in the old Abraham Lincoln Hotel in Springfield.

We went to Chicago where I talked to several groups of women. I remember speaking to a group of about 400, and I was at a loss as to what to say. I told them about farm life and that most of them were probably two or three generations removed from the farm, and wished that they were back. This drew some laughter, and many of the women came to me after the speech and told me about their connection to farm life, including some who had relatives still actively engaged in farming.

From left to right: The author, Richard Ogilvie, U.S. Senator Everett Dirksen, U.S. Senator Charles Percy and Rep. Les Arends

Six of the eight elected state officials, left to right: Alan Dixon, John Lewis, Mike Howlett, Paul Simon, author, Mike Bakalis. Missing: Bill Scott and Richard Ogilvie.

Our campaigning was very successful, and I won the election with a plurality of 250,000 votes. Everett Dirksen and I were the only Republican candidates to carry Cook County. I beat my opponent there by over 20,000 votes. The only statewide candidate that received more votes than I did was Everett Dirksen.

While serving as Clerk of the Supreme Court, I had many rewarding experiences. I went to Washington several times and became well acquainted with President Nixon. I visited the White House on several occasions. Once while I was in the Oval Office, President Nixon got up and told me to have a seat in his chair. That was quite a thrill. I also had breakfast one morning with Henry Kissinger in the Senate Office Building.

My wife and I were given tours of the White House and the south lawn. I was with President Nixon when he planted a Sequoia tree. Every president plants a tree on the White House lawn.

I also went to a meeting that was held in Dolly Madison's house across Lafayette Park from the White house. This was a meeting of Supreme Court Clerks from several states. This meeting led to the development of a national convention of the Supreme Court Clerks from all states. This convention is still active to this day.

I happened to be in Washington on the same day they held the Poor Man's March. There was a crowd of 100,00 people, including individuals with mules and wagons. There were lots of hippies mixed in with other people, and they were smoking marijuana and wading through the pool at the Washington Monument. The smell of marijuana was so strong that it was hard to breathe.

I also had the chance to ride the underground tram from the capitol to the senate office building with Senator Dirksen. He said he was too old to walk that far, so we took the tram. Few people know this train runs between the buildings.

In the fall of 1974, a man named Joe Gibbs quit his term with the legislature. I was asked to run for his office in the general election during the fall of 1974. Once it was announced I was a candidate, a group of women called the Eagle Forum came to see me. They were opposed to the Equal Rights Amendment or ERA, and were encouraging me to take a similar stand. A short time later another group from the National Organization of Women or NOW came to see me. They interviewed me and I told them I was opposed to the ERA. They were upset about this news, and worked very hard against my candidacy. They were relentless, and they distorted the truth about my opinions on issues or even some of the simplest things that I said. I believe I would have been able to do more to help women's rights than the ERA advocates believed. This one issue was the difference and the reason I lost the election. I ran for the legislature again in 1976, but I lost. I never sought another major political office after losing this election.

My last elected office was that of precinct committeeman in Rochester. I served in this position for about 15 years. I had come full circle from a local Rochester office to a statewide office and back again.

Early History of Lincolnland Community College

The Illinois legislature passed an act in 1965 that allowed the organization of community colleges. At this time there were several other states that had community colleges, including California, Iowa, and Michigan. They seemed to be valuable assets to the communities in those states. Our legislators thought that Illinois should also have community colleges.

There were two individuals who brought our attention to the need for a community college in the Springfield area. Scotty Hinton, Sangamon County Superintendent of Schools, and Willis Pickrell, superintendent of schools at Pleasant Plains, suggested that each school district appoint two individuals to serve on a committee whose goal was the preparation of a feasibility study. Scotty Hinton and Willis Pickrell began contacting school districts in Cass, Christian, Logan, Menard, Montgomery, and Sangamon counties to discuss this. I was appointed to represent Rochester on this committee.

A letter, requesting $100 to fund a feasibility study was prepared and sent to each district. When adequate funding was available, a company was hired. Their final report indicated a strong need for a local community college. In 1967, citizens of the school districts voted on a referendum to establish the community college and set a tax rate. This referendum passed and plans were implemented. District 186 in Springfield was not included in the community college district initially, but eventually petitioned for inclusion.

One of the first steps needed to form the college was the election of trustees. Candidates were on the ballot in a special election held in the school districts, comprising the community college. Those elected were Walter Atkins from Ashland, Eldon Greenwood from Chatham, Charlie Long from Waggoner, Richard Stone from Pleasant Plains, J. Kennedy Kincaid Jr. from Athens, Justin Taft from Rochester, and Dr. Kenneth Malmberg from Auburn. Six trustees were farmers, and one was a medical doctor.

During one of our initial meetings, a trustee asked if anyone had been to a community college. When we learned that not one of us had ever seen one, we divided into groups and traveled to California, Florida, and Michigan to visit established campuses. From those trips, we gained valuable information that proved to be essential in developing Lincoln Land Community College, as we know it today.

We looked for building space to rent in Springfield, and finally located two rooms in Illes Park Place. Instead of buying furniture, we rented a table, desk, and chairs. The day the furniture was delivered and the phone was installed was the first day of work for our secretary, Miss Diane Alvies, the first employee of the college. Lincolnland Community College was now open for business.

It was an amusing situation. We had rented rooms and office furniture, and hired a secretary, but there was no business except for a few boxes of notes and minutes from trustee meetings. This situation changed quickly, and she soon needed help to keep up with the volume of work. One of the biggest tasks for the trustees was yet to be completed, hiring a president. The trustees had made a list of criteria to follow throughout the selection process. The process began in earnest in 1967 when we advertised the formation of Lincolnland Community College and an immediate need for a president. The job announcement was circulated throughout the United States, and over 20 applications were received. Eventually, the number of eligible candidates was reduced to five individuals.

Our next step was to interview applicants in their home states. My job was to go to Bakersfield, California with Charlie Long and Kennedy

Kincaid to interview Dr. Robert Poorman. When these preliminary interviews were completed, the finalists were invited to come to Springfield for interviews with the rest of the trustees. The trustees interviewed these applicants at the Sangamo Club in Springfield. Our wives visited with their wives during the interviews, a system that worked very well.

We were highly impressed with Dr. Robert Poorman from California and we offered the position to him. Our secretary, Miss Diane Alvies, became his secretary as well as the first secretary for the president of the college. Later we received a magazine from the Community College Association that contained an article listing criteria for trustees to follow when selecting a president. We were pleased to learn that we had followed all but one or two from the eighty listed. It wasn't bad for a group of trustees that had never been through the process before.

We had one final task before us, and that was the selection of a permanent site for the college campus. Since campus funding was coming from the State of Illinois, we made arrangements to meet with the "State Board of Higher Education" at DeKalb. We flew to the meeting, believing that we were going to learn about finances. Instead, we were surprised when we were told that the final site for the college had been selected by this state board and was to be located next to Sangamon State University, and we didn't have to worry about it any more. That was exactly what we didn't want to hear. This news made Dr. Poorman extremely angry, and he argued with the state board for several minutes. It made no difference. The decision had been made, and the state board controlled the finances. This site is where the college stands today.

Dr. Poorman did an admirable job of starting and organizing the college, but his desire to start classes in the fall of 1968 seemed an impossible task. We could not find any reasonably priced space to rent in Springfield to serve as a temporary campus. Then, a Peoria contractor told us that he could build plywood buildings for the temporary campus and have them ready for use in 90 days, for the same amount of money that we would be required to spend for rent. It was the best solution to our problem. The buildings proved to be durable and a very good value, but their presence caused the nickname "Plywood U" to be applied to the fledgling college. These temporary buildings lasted many years. In fact, two of the plywood structures were moved to the permanent campus and used until recently. With their departure, Lincolnland can no longer be called "Plywood U."

Dr. Poorman served admirably until his retirement in 1988. He took Lincolnland from two rented rooms to a widely recognized community college with over ten thousand students. In retirement he has continued to serve in the field of education as temporary president at several colleges, including one located in Europe.

My final task as trustee of the college was to serve on the committee responsible for hiring the architectural firm to design the buildings of the permanent campus. I was elected as Clerk of the Supreme Court in 1968, so I did not seek re-election as trustee of Lincolnland. I believed that being a trustee and holding a statewide office represented a conflict of interest. State funding was being used for the community college, and I wanted to avoid any potential impropriety. The formation of Lincolnland Community College is one of my greatest accomplishments, and I am proud of my work as trustee during its early years.

Rochester Historical Society

There had never been any historical preservation societies in Rochester until about 1985. At this time, a house in Rochester was being dismantled for a new construction project when it was discovered to be a very early log home. This log house in fact dated back to the very beginnings of Rochester. Many Rochester citizens expressed the thought that the log home should be preserved, so the Rochester Historical Society was formed to assist in the preservation efforts.

The home contained logs that had been used in another building. A name was found on one of the logs and it was determined to be the name of one of the early blacksmiths in Rochester. A plan was developed to dismantle the home and reassemble it at another site. All of the wood appeared to be red oak.

Stone house, circa 1917

The log home preservation caused people to think of another pioneer home in the Rochester area. The stone house located about two and one-half miles east of town was truly a pioneer home and information was available on the builder of the property.

The story of the stone house begins in the year 1834 when Samuel Stevens moved to Rochester from Vermont and began to build a home. Legend has it that Samuel's wife would not come to Illinois until he had built a home like the one they had in Vermont. It would take two years for Samuel to build their home.

He began by purchasing an 80-acre tract of land in the east part of Rochester Township. The site that he selected for building was a knoll that would be free of water problems. He began digging out the soil so the first level of the building would be below ground. This would help with the heating during the winter and would also help keep the home cool during the summer. The first floor of the building would be four feet below ground.

Once all of the dirt had been dug out, a well was dug in the northeast corner of the home. This well was seventeen feet deep. To the rear of the home, Stevens dug a cistern to provide soft water for laundry. Stevens obtained his stone from the Williams Quarry that was located on the South Fork River in the southwest corner of Rochester Township. This is the same quarry that furnished the stone for the old state capital building.

Stevens built two fireplaces in his new home, one on the first level that was partially underground and another on the second floor. The one on the first level had a fireplace crane that held pots for cooking and a small oven was built into one side. This small oven apparently was used for baking bread.

A circular stairway was built from the second floor, to provide access to the third floor. The third floor had a partition that divided the area into two rooms. This floor was probably used for sleeping and would divide the children's side from the parents. A lean-to for tools and other items was built onto the back of the home, and a large porch was constructed on two sides.

The house was completed in 1836 and the Stevens Family or their descendents lived in the home until about the year 1900. Other families occupied the house for another 60 years. Its only use for the next 40 years was hay storage. Time and a lack of maintenance were taking a toll on the building. The roof was beginning to sag and it was obvious that it would soon be in a state of considerable disrepair.

I had known about the old stone house since my childhood. People had talked about its preservation for many years, but nothing ever seemed to get done. When the owners of the property, the Mendenhalls, heard of the preservation interests, they offered to give it to Rochester if they would move it from their farm. The decision was made to accept the home and reassemble it at another location. The preservation began with the recording of detailed notes on the entire house. As the building was dismantled, each piece was numbered to permit its identification at another location. An 1842-penny was found in the cistern during the disassembly.

Citizens belonging to the Rochester Historical Society had raised about $30,000 for the preservation of the stone house. Their efforts were greatly assisted by a grant of $75,000 from the "Illinois First" program. We now had ample funds for the project and we had decided on the location. We succeeded in hiring Wyman Stubbs who is a skilled stonemason. He had worked with his father on the reconstruction and restoration of the old state capital building. He was willing to help us with the work. Reassembly began in the Fall of 2002.

Our plan was to reassemble it just like it was on the farm. We did not dig a well on the inside and the fireplace is lined with firebricks, but the rest of the building is to be reassembled to its original condition. Our efforts reached a milestone on October 18, 2003 when the Masonic Lodge of the State of Illinois placed the cornerstone in the building.

There is no doubt that this building will be standing a hundred years from now. It has walls that are nearly two feet thick in places. It is wonderful to have this building reconstructed for everyone to learn from and enjoy. However, I can't help but wonder what Samuel Stevens would think of the amount of money that we have spent putting his home back together.

Stone house reconstruction in progress, October 18, 2003.

Plans are in place for the log house to be constructed at the same site. Construction is slated to begin in the spring of 2004.

The Rochester Historical Society is also active in keeping alive the history of our early pioneers with annual Cemetery Walks. Volunteer actors in local cemeteries depict individual pioneers. These actors are from the local community and period dress is used as best can be determined. It is hoped that present generations will be enlightened of the accomplishments and hardships of our pioneer fore fathers.

Epilogue

A Tribute to Our Parents

In 1947 Mardell and Justin Taft, Jr. added another budding branch to the Illinois Taft Family Tree with their marriage. Our parents settled on a farm near the village of Rochester, Illinois whose population was then 400 people. The newlyweds moved into a house built by our paternal grandparents in 1929. This white wood-frame bungalow was first a home to our Taft grandparents where they successfully raised their four children through the years of economic depression and World War II. Dad was six-years-old when his family first inhabited their new home and, in contrast to present-day norms, our father remained under that same roof for the next seventy-three years and continues to do so until this day.

Our mother and father became proud parents of five healthy children over the course of thirteen years, from 1948 to 1961. Collectively, the brood consisted of three boys and two girls. Chronologically, our singular birth order was: George, Jim, Nancy, Justin III, and Carolyn. We were each born with a strong sense of place and origin that stemmed from the firm network of roots first established by Taft's in Sangamon County in 1828. Growing up during the 1950s and 1960s in this agricultural heartland town gave us all a sense of community and instilled in us the core values that make up the backbone of America. We were allowed to ride bikes and run with our friends without fear of anything happening to us. Everyone knew everyone else and we all looked out for each other.

Our parents have been exceptional role models. Our mother is a Registered Nurse. She graduated in 1947 from Memorial Hospital School of Nursing in Springfield, Illinois and began her career working in a local doctor's office. When the family grew she chose to stay home with her children. After her youngest child was born in 1961 she returned to work as a private duty nurse, working the night shift so she could be home during the day and evening hours. During the 1970s she was the Director of Nursing for Americana Nursing Center and Lewis Memorial Christian Village, both in Springfield, Illinois. In the early 1980s she became the Administrator of the Eastern Star Home in Macon, Illinois. She then went to work for the State of Illinois as a first-aid nurse. Her work allowed the family to have many extras in life.

The house we grew-up in, as it looked in 1962

Our father graduated in 1941 from Rochester High School as valedictorian of his senior class. Years later, when prodding his children to excel academically, Dad would occasionally remind us of his laudable high school performance. As we grew older, we discovered the fact that his senior class had only consisted of seventeen students...so in good-natured humor we would remind him of that fact during these fatherly 'pep-talks'. Of course, no one was that foolishly impertinent in the face of any real scholarly infraction.

Dad attended the University of Illinois in Champaign-Urbana from 1941 to 1943, where he found a stimulating environment in which he thrived. During that time he was a member of the Alpha Gamma Rho agricultural fraternity and paid his own tuition and board by working in the university livestock barns. He was also a member of the U of I Livestock Judging Team. Dad has regaled us with many stories of campus life. Due to the onset of an unexpected illness experienced by Grandfather Taft, he returned home in 1943 to help his dad and assume responsibility for operating the family farm. He continued to run the farm until 1968. Our father has a natural ability to tell a joke and to generally socialize with anybody he meets. This gift of loquacious affability led him into community service at a young age, first at the local level, then the county and statewide levels. We all have memories of our father attending community meetings. He was elected president of the school board at 33 years of age. In 1958, he was elected township supervisor. As we grew, he became involved at the county level, holding two elected positions. In 1968, he was elected to the statewide position of Clerk of the Illinois Supreme Court. Through all of the campaigns and chicken dinners, we grew to appreciate the need to participate in the political process and to contribute to our community.

Our parents have big hearts, especially toward friends. Each of us had a friend who was made to feel like part of the family, often calling our house their second home. In a couple of instances, our parents allowed a friend whose family life was not as fortunate as ours to live with us. Several of these friends are still considered as part of our family to the present time. In testimony to our parent's open hearts and generosity, some of these individuals have since reciprocated by donating free skills and materials from their present livelihood to benefit their 'adopted parents'.

The dinner hour was always a lively event in our home. You never knew beforehand how many people would be present. Dinner was served to whoever was around at the appointed hour. Food was simply extended to the amount needed to feed the number of persons seated at the table. Guests were always served first, sometimes to the detriment of us children. For example, one of Dad's long-time friends dropped in just as the family was ready to dig into homemade shortcake and ice cream with garden fresh strawberries. Strawberry shortcake was Justin III's (J.T.) favorite dessert. Much to his chagrin his portion was minimized in order to serve our unexpected guest. This sacrifice of his part became one of many family jokes over time. The dinner hour always entailed lively discussion. Our father consistently explained current events and politics to us in easily understandable terms. This included both world and local topics and we were expected to contribute to the discourse with questions and opinions. However, the dinner conversation was not always so lofty. More often topics included: what happened at school for each of us, how we spent our playtime, settlement of sibling disputes (a common conflict arose from who ate off the *gray*??! melamac plate) and upcoming family activities. Most family meals were interrupted when someone knocked on the door for our father. This meal interruption was a custom that extended to dining out in restaurants as our father was naturally inclined to navigate the entire restaurant visiting with anyone he could engage in conversation.

Mother and father's dedication to community was part of the fabric of our everyday life. Mom expressed this both socially and as a nurse. Our mother was a proud member of the American Red Cross, which in the 1940s and throughout the 1950s enrolled RNs in a quasi national 'reserve-corps' of nurses in the event of prospective military actions or disasters. As a nurse, mom acted in collaboration with several local physicians and pharmacists to care for many members of our community. By providing local access to healthcare, many people received treatment that otherwise would not. Her treatment also mitigated the cost and the ten-mile travel distance required for a doctor's office visit in Springfield. Our family's home kitchen served as a makeshift clinic where Mom would receive guidance or verbal orders via telephone from the local physician based upon her assessment of the patient. Her services included: triage, blood pressure readings, vaccinations, antibiotic and allergy injections, wound dressing, creating splints and slings, applying elastic bandages and clarifying oral medication schedules – plus other miscellaneous skills. Our refrigerator had one upper shelf dedicated to strange vials of medications, which were mysteriously kept in a locked container off limits to children. The present day healthcare environment discourages any such overture due to fear of lawsuits.

Through different routes of action, our father provided us with a living example of community service. As the Rochester Township Supervisor it became a daily occurrence to have people in need knock on our door for assistance. In 1958 this assistance was called 'relief'. Whoever answered the door ran and got Dad, whereupon he would visit with whoever asked for relief assistance. Dad always made a point of getting acquainted with people and in the process showed that he cared about their life struggles and needs without passing judgment upon them. In fulfillment of his role as township supervisor, Dad would write out a requisition that was accepted at any grocery store as legal tender in exchange for food. This process was similar to the food stamps currently distributed by government programs, but the face-to-face local interaction is now absent. It's hard to say that our present system is an improvement. Today people of lesser means are labeled as indigents and it is harder to qualify for public assistance, as evidenced by America's growing population of homeless people.

One story we all remember took place before Christmas of 1960. As usual, a man came to our backdoor and explained to Dad that due to a recent financial setback he was unable to provide his family with Christmas dinner that year. Since the man worked at a local nursery, he assured Dad that our trees would be trimmed in exchange for this needed relief. Dad understood the awkwardness of his embarrassed state. Dad repeatedly told the man that he was not personally giving him anything, but that it was only within his elected capacity that he wrote this requisition for groceries. He also let him know that while he appreciated his offer to trim our trees, it was not part of the transaction and reiterated that local government gave the relief. Alas, this message seemed to fall on deaf ears. On Christmas day our family went to Aunt Helen Burch's house for the celebratory turkey dinner. As the festivities concluded, we all piled back into our 1959 turquoise ninety-eight Oldsmobile and headed toward home. As we turned into our driveway a sudden gasp was emitted by our mother, followed by equal expressions of disbelief from the rest of us. Our mature trees and bushes that normally filled our yard and framed our home had been so severely trimmed that they were nearly bald! Dad said we were never to say a word about it because the trees and bushes would grow back over time.

Our father also served as the Secretary-Treasurer of the Rochester Cemetery. Dad's role in this capacity also impacted our daily life by consequent events that seemed normal at the time to we children. For example, it was not unusual to go up to the Rochester Post Office to get our family mail and be directed by the Postmaster to sign a registered receipt for a cremated body that was to be buried in the cemetery. More often, Dad's involvement with the local cemetery was expressed by a multitude of phone calls involving the purchase of lots, notification of a death, the need to dig a grave or interface with Wilson Park's Funeral Home in Rochester or the tombstone businesses. The Rochester Cemetery was created on land donated by our great grandfather, William Taft. As a consequence, Dad was to 'keeper of the scrolls' as we kids called it. These canvas 'scrolls' were actually the only documented map that provided a reference of who was buried in what lot location. Through our father's continued effort and sustained commitment to the cemetery, he arranged in the 1970s to have the cemetery ownership to be passed on to the Rochester

Township. That transaction ensured the existence and maintenance of the cemetery for all the community in future years.

Our mother and father both strongly encouraged patriotism or love of our country. This value were not limited to the public arena for political gain, but was quietly transmitted at home. In particular, the Fourth of July was a special holiday in our home. One of our family photo albums contains a picture of the entire family in the front yard in a circle around the flagpole. The eldest son, George, is playing his coronet as Dad raises the flag according to regulation and the rest of the family is standing with erect posture and right hand over their heart. There is certainly an atmosphere of respect communicated to the viewer in this photograph. The Fourth of July was also greatly celebrated in the village of Rochester by parades, carnivals, barbecues and fireworks. The events lasted all day and our family served in different roles required to make the day a community success.

These are just a few stories and reflections that we recall while growing up in the household of Justin and Mardell Taft. As you can imagine, there are many more. With five children and very active parents, there was never a dull moment at our house. During our childhood, we heard many of the stories recounted by our father in this book. Each of us long encouraged our father to write his stories down so that future Taft generations and other interested people can enjoy them. We are pleased and proud that he has done so. We hope that you enjoy them as much as we do!

Respectfully, your children,

George E. Taft
James R. Taft
Nancy J. (Taft) Semenza
Justin Taft III
Carolyn M. (Taft) Grosboll

Biography Of Justin Taft

The author

Justin Taft was born in Rochester, Illinois on January 29, 1924. Mr. Taft was educated in the Rochester schools and attended the University of Illinois. After his college years, he returned to operate his family farm that was settled by his ancestors in 1828 when they came to Illinois from Vermont.

He is a member of the Alpha Gamma Rho Fraternity, Masonic Order, Consistory and Shrine, Past Patron O. E. S.: 4-H Club leader for ten years; member Isaac Walton League; Past President of the Rochester School Board; Past Chairman local United Fund Drives;. Was named "Outstanding Young Farmer of Sangamon County in 1959. He is a member of the Rochester Christian Church; Springfield Lions Club; past member Springfield Junior Chamber of Commerce; member of planning Board of Lincoln Land Community College, Springfield and served three years on the founding Board of Trustees of that College.

Elected Rochester Township Supervisor in 1959, he served in this capacity until his election as Probate Clerk of Sangamon County in 1962. He was appointed Under Sheriff of Sangamon County in 1966. In 1968 he was elected to the office of Clerk of the Illinois Supreme Court.

Mr. Taft is married to the former Mardell Kieffer of Loami, Illinois. They have five children, George, James, Nancy, Justin III, and Carolyn.

Printed in the United States
16711LVS00003B/148-228